U

Potential

Run the Best Race of Your Life

Genesis Hey Krick

ISBN -13: 978-1978279513
ISBN -10: 1978279515

Dedicated to you—and your success!

I want to acknowledge and thank:

God—for giving me the opportunities in my life to help others and to be in the place I am today. I could not have done it on my own.

My mother—for the advice, the empowerment, the love and the devotion; for helping me get back up after I had fallen over and over and over again.

My father—for the help and guidance in completing my first book. It was a huge undertaking and he pushed me to create the greatest product possible. I thank him for pushing me to be the best, not just in writing this book, but in life.

My brothers—for always being a part of all my endeavors, and sticking with me through thick and thin.

My loving grandmother, Roxy—for always believing in me and encouraging me no matter how hard or challenging life has gotten.

My amazing friend, Candin—a lifelong friend, who struggled with me, took the leap of faith to move to California, and has always been there for me.

My great encourager, Reverend Stevie Craft—for

keeping me on track and always reminding me of the "living truth."

CONTENTS

Foreword – James Malinchak

Introduction

1   Finding Your Purpose   1

2   Choose to Believe You Can   32

3   Happy with Where You are Heading?   41

4   Never Give Up, Ever!   72

5   Getting to Know the Real You   84

6   Mission, Vision, Values   108

7   Creating Your Plan of Action   129

8   How to Implement Your Goals   163

9   Enjoying the Ride   180

10 Taking Smart Risks   193

11 Tools that You Didn't Learn in School   208

12   Failure vs. Triumph   220

    Bio   240

"Sooner or later, those who win are

those who think they can."

—**Richard Bach**

FOREWORD

You may remember me from being featured on the hit ABC TV show, "Secret Millionaire." If you do not know of the show, here is the basic premise from show promotions:

"What happens when business motivational speaker and self-made millionaire James Malinchak is picked up by an ABC television crew, placed on an airplane with no money, credit cards, cell phone, laptop or watch, and is whisked off to an impoverished neighborhood, where he had to survive on $44.66 cents for a week?

The show features Malinchak leaving his current lifestyle in search of real-life heroes who are making a difference in their local community. He ultimately reveals himself as a millionaire and rewards them with a portion of his own money to further their cause by gifting them with checks of his own money totaling over $100,000. If you watched ABC's 'Secret Millionaire' you know that James is no ordinary entrepreneur. He is a self-made millionaire with a strong passion for giving back and serving others."

Amazingly, over 10 MIILLION people watched me

on the show! Whether I am speaking at a conference, walking through an airport, consulting for an entrepreneur or just hanging out at a coffee shop, I always seem to get asked the same question. "What was it like being on Secret Millionaire when you had to live undercover in an impoverished neighborhood and how did it affect you?"

My answer is always the same.

The greatest gift you can have is when you simply give in order to help and serve others. There is no better feeling than when you know you have made a positive difference in the lives of others.

And that is <u>exactly</u> what my friend Genesis Hey Krick and her teachings can do for you! She will inspire you through sharing her wisdom and personal experiences.

Genesis is an author, speaker and leader who truly cares about making a positive difference in the lives of others.

In this book you will be inspired by her genuine, caring nature for making a difference in your life.

And her strategies can help you to achieve more than ever before.

Some strategies may comfort you while others may challenge your old paradigm. One thing is for certain. Genesis and her strategies will stamp your spirit with an abundance of love, hope and encouragement so you can reach new levels of courage, fulfillment and personal happiness.

It is my sincere honor to introduce to you Genesis and her amazing book!

- James Malinchak

Featured on ABCs Hit TV Show, *"Secret Millionaire"*

Authored 20 Books, Presenter and Consultatant
Best-Selling Author, *Millionaire Success Secrets*
Founder of www.MillionaireFreeBook.com

INTRODUCTION

You have great potential, but your goal needs a plan, or it doesn't move beyond being just a dream. You already believe in it, but now to succeed, you have to put it into action. That's where I come in—I want to help you claim your talent, reach for your dreams, and *unleash your potential*.

Your amazing future awaits! We all know that five years is a long time, especially if you are young, but I want you to start thinking ahead. For your personal growth, it is necessary to have a forward thinking mindset.

If you ask yourself, "Where will I be five years from now?" What would you say? Can you answer, "I know exactly what I want to do, and I can tell you exactly what direction I am headed. . ."?

Maybe you could tell me where you want to be by that time, but can you determine exactly *how* you will get there? Once you decide where, then you realize that there has to be a way to get to *any* destination point.

Remember, for every circumstance you have experienced, there has been an occurrence that led you there—a deliberate choice, an unplanned event, your action or inaction, that influences outcome. It doesn't matter the current state of affairs you find yourself in, because it is *never* too late to make a positive change—or too early! You are on this earth for a purpose, and that purpose is to live out your life ambitions—follow your dreams and make a difference!

I am sure there are a number of you who feel you have no idea where you are headed. Uncertainty is fine for some people and some seasons of life, but if *you* are here reading this book, you have realized that fresh direction and change are exactly what you have been looking for. What I share with you throughout this book can be applied in a business startup or a creative venture; and for personal transformation, professional and personal development, and so much more.

As you personally apply the knowledge you gain throughout this book, opportunities will manifest into your life that you never thought possible, not even in your wildest dreams! This book is a step-by-step guide, which, when put into action in your life, will provide you the tools for success and dramatically enhance your life.

What are *my* goals for you? 1) To give you proven tools to increase your awareness about making educated decisions. These include: how to prioritize and set goals for strategic planning, which increases your clarity by identifying what it is you really want out of your life. 2) Help you discover your vision and purpose, and develop a plan of action to achieve them. 3) Learn how to be comfortable networking with anyone, as you build strong relationships in both your business and personal life. Formulate leadership skills, as you begin to see yourself jumping ahead of the learning curve—and so much more! My goal is to simply provide you with the map and the compass; you just have to commit to walking the path forward, my friend. . .   Get ready! Welcome to a the best race of your life—there are incredible surprises ahead as you advance onward to achieve what you are meant to do. Be prepared to get a fast jump out of the starting blocks, or leaping out of the box that you have been confined—and enjoy watching yourself grow into the person you are meant to become. I am very excited for you, and feel privileged that you have chosen me to be your guide as you take each adventurous step forward.

"If you set goals and go after them with all the determination you can muster, your gifts will take you places that will amaze you." —Les Brown

Genesis Hey Krick M.A, CLC
Expert in Leadership, Development, and Entrepreneurship – Founder of the Shine On Network

CHAPTER 1

FINDING YOUR PURPOSE

Every single day brings you new opportunities. There's no turning back, so let's dig in and get you where you want to be tomorrow. Have you ever wanted to accomplish something so badly that you could almost taste, smell, and feel exactly what it is you are trying to reach? Have you ever felt that you were destined for greatness? I have a news flash for you. You are ordained for more than just greatness, my friend—you were designed for victory!

You can be set free from whatever has been holding you back in your life. I want to help release you from any limiting feelings or form of bondage, so that you are able to live your ultimate life purpose. I know that there are many of you who really don't have a clue what you are supposed to do in your life, much less

recognize an ordained purpose. Life purpose comes in all shapes and sizes so don't
worry, because with the help of this book I am
going to help you figure it out. By the time
you are finished reading, my ultimate goal is
for you to be able to live a more fulfilling life
by making what you learn in this book count—
and ultimately gratify your purpose!

The first clue about your life purpose is to
recognize your passions and natural gifts.
What is it you love? Your greater purpose begins when you start making each day count by
taking deliberate steps towards your goal—not
just talking about it, or telling yourself, why
not, but by creating tangible meaning for your
life with positive action forward. And as you
do so, you will see your one passion or perceived direction becomes multifaceted. For
example, I am an entrepreneur and business
coach, an expert in organizational leadership,
a motivational speaker and author. My all-
around purpose became clear after traveling
and experiencing different paths, which
helped point the way to my ultimate purpose,
fulfilling my core passions—even so, there's
always more to learn—*so much more!* T h e
time is now my friend, for you to make a
choice and commit yourself to creating a new

beginning. By opening this book, you made a conscious decision to no longer wait around for change to come to you. You have decided that you are going to be proactive and direct your mindset into a focused and positive direction. You have the ability to change your life and you have the ability to *do it now!* No matter what card you have been dealt up until this point, you can feel confident in knowing that "where there is a will there is a way!"

I am excited and you will be too, because we are going to make tracks quickly so that you can create changes immediately. The most important thing you can do is to stick with me. Pretend I am your running partner, and we are in a marathon together. Do not let me get out of your sight! I will not give up on you and you can't give up on me because we are a team from here on out! Every time you feel like giving up, remember that there are incredible opportunities that are awaiting you; and you cannot afford *to not* go after them. If you stay right next to me in this race you will do tremendously well! In this thing called life, I want you to be a strong competitor. Hope you've got it? Good! Before we dive in, head first, I would like to tell you a little bit about myself so you are not wondering where I came from and who I am. I want this to be a personal relationship where you can feel comfortable in knowing that I was in your exact shoes for a long time. How do I know that's true? Because it is part of the human condition and part of life. I have been lost, confused, frustrated, upset, depressed, angry, everything you can possibly imagine. I have been able to overcome many obstacles in my life, and will share with you what I have learned. My lessons learned may shorten your learning curve, and you won't make the same mistakes that I did.

I am originally a small town girl, born and raised in Dixon, Illinois. My family's quaint little place in Dixon was the perfect place to grow up. It was very difficult to ever leave it, because I had many wonderful memories with family and friends. As a child, growing up on thirteen acres of wooded land, I was able to be completely free-spirited, having the best time of my life, with no worries. There were divine blackberries to feast on, ripe red and green apples, fresh off the tree, and delicious honey from our hard-working bees, along with gorgeous planted flowers in every color you can imagine. At night, when the stars came out, the sky was bright with twinkling stars, and we would stand back and look at it in wonder. I loved our land; it was a beautiful place to grow up, but I knew that I could not stay there forever, because I had big dreams to pursue. As I got older, I began to feel a burning desire to do something out of the ordinary, something special to change people's lives, but I didn't know what that was. It took a lot of thought and I had a very difficult time deciphering what I could do to help figure it out. After all, there are so many areas in which people need help, and like many others, I ultimately wanted to save the world.

My front yard in Dixon

In my late teens, narrowing down "saving the world" was a difficult task, because how could I pick just one thing? The last thing I thought about, unfortunately, was my education. I was an all around athlete and loved sports. Track, to me, was my life and there was nothing more important than running in the race, crossing that finish line and winning. I can recall the day of my last track meet in high school where I was in place to run the 400 meter dash at "Sectionals" and I was to run against two of the fastest girls in our state. If you are aware of Illinois state track, you are knowledgeable about the fact that we have one of the most competitive state competitions in the United States.

The whole day I had severe anxiety, because I knew this would be the last time I would run the 400 meter dash. It was also my last chance to prove myself and to do my very best. My goal was to make it to the state competition.

That evening, the time had finally come where I stepped into the blocks. It was quite surreal because I knew this could be it. . . I knelt down to the blocks, and everything started to slow down. I closed my eyes, started praying to God that he would give me the strength to succeed, stretched out my numb legs, and took several heavy breaths as I carefully stepped into the blocks. The night was chilly and I can remember seeing my breath while I exhaled. I saw the man with the gun step up to the line, and I said to myself that this was my last chance to make it happen! All of a sudden, the shot rang out and I busted out of the blocks, my adrenaline was screaming! With every step I pushed myself farther and farther ahead, with my arms swinging wildly in rhythm, and my mind more focused than ever before. The crowd was cheering and hollering, but I could not hear them, I was so focused in my head that all I could hear was my breathing. Just breathe, I thought, *just control my breathing.*

If you are not familiar with the 400 meter dash, it is one of the most challenging races to run, because it is very difficult to pace yourself. A person has to give it their ALL the entire race!

I rounded the corner of the 200 and I was still in first, and I knew I just had to keep this place—*just hold, I thought, you can do this!* All of a sudden, near the 300 mark I felt one of the girls whiz by me like a flash, and then another—and I thought, *Genesis you are going to make it— pick it up!* I had 100 left, that's all!

Running my heart out, I gave everything I had and left it on the track!

Run Genesis run! I pushed and struggled, my legs felt like jelly, and I saw my life flashing before my eyes! 50 left, 10 left. All the while, I heard people yelling! It was a photo finish; I crossed the line and desperately looked over. . . I realized that I had not gotten first or second, which is what I needed to go to state.

Frantically out of breath I asked the timer, "What's my time!" He looked down at the watch and then looked back at me and said, "You're going to state, you qualified!" I couldn't believe it, I had made it! I did it! I jumped up and down, more excited than you can imagine. All that was left was the announcement, and it would be confirmed that I was going to state. I sat there anticipating it, waiting eagerly. Suddenly, the man's voice started echoing through the track. To my dismay, when he made the announcement over the loudspeaker, he stated that according to the times there were only two women who had qualified for the 400. I ran straight up to the box and asked what was going on. They stated, "Sorry sweetie, you were *one tenth off*; the timer at the line was just a bit off."
I stepped back utterly devastated, and heartbroken. This couldn't be happening to me, I was told that I could go! I ran out of the box

office sobbing my eyes out. I was crushed! I had worked so hard my entire life to get to this point. I threw myself under a tree and felt that life itself could no longer go on. While I was sitting in despair, my mom came up to me, and put her arms around me and said "Gen, it's okay. . . You want to know why? Because you gave it your all, you could not have given any more than you did on that track, every bit of energy, every bit of dedication, your whole heart and personal devotion was left on that track." And then she smiled and added, "By the way, you ran the best time of your life."

I looked up into her kind eyes staring at me; I thought about that statement for a minute—and immediately it soaked in as such an important life lesson. In life, we don't always get what we want, and aren't awarded a win. But when we give it our absolute all, people know it—and I knew it, even if it didn't work out the way I planned. You know it when you've given it your absolute all, too.

I learned, right then, that it was important to live life with this attitude, *always giving it my all*. We can live as a winner, regardless of outcomes or circumstances. It is important to adopt this attitude: *Live life by giving your all, at all times!* If you live your life this way, you will never look back and say that you should have tried harder, you should have given more, you should have believed more, or you should have given it something different. No regrets, because you already did all that you could! I am proud to say that from that day forward I always looked at life differently. We all go through trials and hardships, *but knowing that you are always trying your best gives you an incredible sense of peace in your heart.* The reason that I told you this story is not only to give you a little bit more insight into who I am as a person, but to also speak to you about how experiences can affect people. <u>We cannot allow disappointments, heartache, or perceived unfairness to keep us in bondage, keeping us a victim to it</u>. We can't live yesterday again—we don't get do-overs, except by using what we've learned to benefit what we choose to do today.

Any one of us can go through terrible circumstances and not understand how to handle them. We can live in the past and forget about our future. We can forget about our passions and our purpose, and then disregard the things that are most important to living a fulfilling life.

I am here to tell you that now is the time

to make a change in your mindset, your life-style and the way you live. Acknowledge to yourself that you are ready to run the best race of your life, put everything you've got on the track! The old adage, "Nothing worthwhile comes easy," is true! You can gain and attain a positive mindset even in the most difficult of times. Regardless of where you currently are in your life, change is good and it can take you to places you never thought possible. So, get ready to learn, alter, shift, and trans-form—enabling you to *unleash your potential!*

To fast forward a bit: I decided when I went to college that I would move to the big city—Chicago—and see what experiences it held. Little did I know there's a lot more to city living than meets the eye? <—is this a question?) It was night and day from the se-cure, pristine, thirteen acres where I grew up. I was used to birds chirping in the apple or-chard out my bedroom window, but in Chica-go, I woke to screeching tires and horns blar-ing. It took some getting used to. I was at-tending Lewis University, accepted on a track scholarship, which was incredibly exciting to me, since running track was always my first love, in addition to time with friends and fam-ily.   I n college, I only performed track competitively for one year, because over that year I realized it was no longer my primary focus and purpose. However, I still didn't know what I wanted to do, but I knew I needed to figure it out soon. I'm sure you know kids (maybe you are one) who wait until their junior year, or the last possible minute to make a decision about what to major in, in school. Well, I was one of them. I couldn't imagine myself doing *only one* thing for the rest of my life. I changed my mind about five times before I actually made a decision about declaring my major. I finally chose marketing, one of the broadest degrees that one can attain. I thought at least if I do something that's broad, it will keep a lot of doors open in case I change my mind down the road. I finished my degree after four years, only to find out there were no jobs available because so many individuals had a marketing degree, or so it seemed. I looked everywhere, and found no job; I couldn't seem to get hired without experience. I was frustrated beyond belief and thought, "How am I going to pay to live here?" I couldn't move back to Dixon, because who would hire a marketer in a town of less than fifteen thousand people? Small businesses don't really need marketing, or so I thought.

Let me ask you this question... one I had to ask myself. "What do you do if you feel that you have no options and you're stuck?" Let me remind you that you *always* have options. Please hear this loud and clear: **There is not a single situation in life in which you are not able to make a choice. Don't fool yourself by accepting the lie that you have no choice. False!**

If you think that you have exhausted all of your options, *think harder.* Sometimes it takes thinking outside the box, and gaining a new and fresh perspective, to grasp what you need to do to take the next step forward. No cramps, no stalling, no falling down, no giving up. Never say never! Stay in the race, because there is always a need that other people are not providing that you can meet with your passion and talents—this puts your purpose into action. Think outside the box; it provokes thoughts that are not currently being considered. *After all, being unconventional is a source for invention!* If you look at a situation and it does not seem as though there is a way to sort out a resolution to get where you want to go, or be what you want to be, I encourage you to look at the scenario from a completely different standpoint. Consider every possibility until you know for a fact it can't be done. Make this thought process a natural element of your lifestyle. Only when all possibilities are considered, do you then evolve to the next action step. And this is not giving up. In fact, it is quite the opposite; *it's simply modifying your original concept of how living your purpose looks.* This includes staying fluid and flexible in thought and action.

I want you to implement this "outside of

the box" concept, every day, no matter what life brings to you. I want you to be able to get comfortable with the uncomfortable. I am not recommending this to make you nervous; I am suggesting it to broaden your horizons, so that you may seize opportunities when they are right in front of your face. I can tell you from experience, most people walk away from risky or fearful situations when they are staring them right in their face. Please hear this: These are the risks that will allow you to get ahead in life. Sometimes you have to take two steps back in order to take three steps forward. For example, imagine at a party, you see this individual who is very successful and you have the opportunity to talk to him or her, you need to go for it! Do not wait or feel insecure about approaching, because you may never again get that same chance to say what you want to say or do what you need to do.

This brings me back to a time when I had the opportunity to see Jay Leno live and be on the set for one of his tapings. My seat was in the front row where I could see everything up close and personal. Every show he offers the opportunity for guests to come up and take a picture with him. Only a select few are witty enough to run forward, and they are the lucky ones who get the opportunity. I remember the golden moment when he asked the question, "Who wants to come up for a picture?" For some reason I hesitated; I lost my shining moment. Within a quick instant, there were three others that made their way to the front. He took an individual picture with each person, and then had them take a seat so he could move on with the show. I was too late and I had missed out! I was so bummed. Why didn't I get up and go!?

I made it a point to learn from this and to never again default on an opportunity that was right in front of my face. Talk about being disappointed. A small part of me thought I might have a chance to do it again, but it wasn't likely. And then within a few months I left LA, and moved back to the Midwest. I realized when I saw his last episode on T.V. that I would never again get that chance. Sometimes, life happens like that; we are only given one chance, so it is important to seize it, or it's a golden opportunity gone.

Shifting gears a bit, think about this for a minute—one important connection may open multiple doors for you, simply because you decided to have the courage to speak up and introduce yourself. I personally have experienced times when I could have, should have, would have opened my mouth—but I didn't. Afterwards, I felt as though I had made a huge mistake. If I would have just politely spoken up, even to say "Hi," it could have made a significant difference. Please understand that *"connections are the key,"* for anything that you do in your life. Whether you're having a one-on-one conversation or you are speaking to a large audience, it's important to make a connection with others! This especially goes for any situation in which you are looking for opportunities—watch for the unexpected ones, then respectfully approach the people who may hold the key. You can choose to take deliberate action to help create opportunity and change for yourself.

I want you to think about this very moment; right here and right now, think about what is right in front of you. Your conscious decision is needed, along with your personal commitment to reach for positive change.

I want you to write below: *"I am committed to making a powerful change in my life. Starting right now this change will begin to enhance my personal growth."* Now, write the date. . .

D A T E :

_____

Good I am so glad we are on the same page. 🙂 You are now on to the next step, my friend. Studies have shown that actually writing down your thoughts of action is a lot more effective than just thinking them. All you need to move forward in action is the correct mindset, and part of that mindset is identifying the time is NOW! And that is something most people have a hard time accepting. Is that you? If so, you may have found it easier to continue putting off what you need to accomplish. Are you a procrastinator?

Think about it like this and see if it sounds familiar? You're sitting at home on the couch watching a movie and you are so comfortable, not to mention you just had the most fantastic dinner and you don't feel like going anywhere. Well, you promised yourself that you were going to the gym, but you don't feel like it. Guess what ladies and gentlemen, this is not rocket science, you need to get off that butt and go!

Making yourself commit to something of value is going to help you be accountable to not only yourself, but to those around you who are counting on you to do your part. I know for me, if I don't make it a point to take initiative on tasks that need to be accomplished, then I can very easily forgo my biggest priorities when setting goals, or even worse, fall back into old habits.

A lot of what we want in our lives we expect to happen *to us*. This is not how the world works, unfortunately, and it is completely unrealistic. As my good friend James Malinchak says, *"Sitting in a lotus position and just hoping that something is going to happen to you, will not guarantee you any results."* You need to make a consistent effort to work towards the specific change that you ultimately want to achieve in your life. The more specific you are about what you want, and why, the easier it will be for you to get there! Through clarity and identification of what you want, you can begin to work towards it, formulating your methods to reach your goals each day.

There was a time that I thought I knew precisely what I wanted, and I was sure that it would be a cake walk to get it. Reason being, I thought I had everything planned out perfectly. I had myself convinced that success was right around the corner. Now, I am the first one to tell you that anything you want in life that involves creating success is challenging. It takes some individuals longer than others to implement their goals, because they have a difficult time staying on track. Succeeding involves many difficult decisions and choices. To name a few: You need to be able to take rejection, and accept falling back. You must be a lifelong learner and be able to identify changing factors that influence your goals and outcomes—over and over again. The good news is that the experience you gain from failures will be utilized as strengths in the future! I know, at times, this seems so difficult to imagine, but trust me; some of the greatest setbacks can become your most amazing testimonials, and the driving force of how to overcome adversity.

There are a number of things that I am going to request of you to help you start making changes. These ideas have made such a tremendous difference for me, so I am excited to share them with you to help you succeed.

Aligning Goals and Priorities

Think about how your goals currently align with your priorities. If they are not aligned, then I suggest you consider making some adjustments. When working with clients, I always recommend they list their top five goals and then list their top five priorities. I then ask them to be realistic in assessing if these line up with each other. If there is no congruency, I help them rework their focus and determine workable outcomes for what they are trying to achieve.

It is beneficial for you to determine your top five goals and priorities, to help you get reasonably clear on where you are headed at this point. You can make adjustments along the way. Remember, **goals (your aim or desired result for your effort)** should be as specific as possible—and **priorities, (the order in which things are important to you)** should be listed from 1 – 5, so you see what you are currently focused on at this time. Such as: taking care of my children, working out four times a week, meeting with one new client a day, etc.

TOP 5 GOALS

1.)_____

2.)_____

_____

3.)_____

_____

4.)_____

_____

5.)_____

_____

TOP 5 PRIORITIES

1.)_____

_____

2.)_____

_____

3.)_____

_____

4.)_____

_____

5.)_____

_____

As you look at what was written you may see that some of the goals and priorities intermix while others don't. Try not to get caught up in making sure they are identically matched, but rather focus on there being a commonality between the two areas. In other words, make sure that your goals and priorities share life intentions with the other area—and that they blend together, and in some way complement each other or ignite your passion.

The next thing we are going to do is work on disciplining your mind to take ACTION! **With your ultimate goal for change in mind**, **let's start with three things that you are going to implement every single day.** While you start thinking about these things, your new thought process will help you to start performing them on a daily basis. A little tidbit I learned while making changes and transitioning in my life is that it takes twenty-one days to form a habit. Knowing this will encourage you to keep things in perspective and help you monitor what changes are being implemented. Obviously, these commitments should coincide with the direction which you want to improve and work toward. Moving on to how you create successful endeavors through action; think about and highlighted three things that you plan to achieve every day. **The number one task/goal should be achieved** no matter what it takes to do so, because you want to be able to make progress, even if it is just an ounce. Some examples of making progress day to day would be: writing two hours each day; comparison research about your type of business; taking time to work out, or self care, even if it only for fifteen minutes, or possibly working on a portion of a large project and putting the rest aside for tomorrow or a designated later date. *Even if you are unable to get to the other two goals every day, make sure you are able to complete the first*. Again, the number one task/ goal should be a definite achievement.

Next, I want you to set a time, and establish an effective environment where you will accomplish your task. For example, if you are working on completing a book, give yourself adequate space; make sure you establish a comfortable setting to work, so that you may accomplish the task efficiently. Set a specific time in your day to complete it. If necessary, set aside your other tasks that you will complete at a later time. In my case, I know that I need to stay off shopping sites when I am writing; otherwise I never finish my writing content for the day.

Learn to create purpose as well. What is the reason—the motivation behind wanting to perform and complete that specific task each day? Now, as you make a personal commitment to accomplish daily tasks/goals, make your time worthwhile by <u>prioritizing</u>—determine what tasks are *most* important. As you develop this step of strategic planning, you will gain personal structuring skills that fit into your aspirations.

As listed above, refer back to your top five priorities. Consider if those priorities need to be changed or adjusted to fit your goals. **Now, please list the three goals you will begin to take action on and accomplish on a daily basis and list them in order of importance:** The reason I say WILL is because you need to take control of your mind and make a decision to implement these every single day. I want you to write these three things also somewhere outside this book so that you can see them clearly, whether it be a poster in your room, on the refrigerator, or another visual location. Remember, doing something for twenty-one days straight helps it become a habit. These goals should be very clear and specific. They should give you a reason to wake up in the morning. Another thing to consider is that <u>these can be three very different types of tasks/goals or they can be</u>

<u>goals focused on the same project or vision</u>.

1.

2.

3.

Now, what about the discipline it takes to follow your course of action? I recently went to a motivational seminar where I heard Anthony Hopkins speak. He is one of my all time favorite actors, and it was such a privilege to not only see him in person, but receive his expertise. There was one thing that he said to the audience which really hit home for me. Someone asked him, "If an individual is trying to pursue an acting career, or any other career for that matter, what is one thing that you could recommend, or the one piece of advice that you would give to that person?"

Anthony stated "Well, what really helped

me was my *mindset,* and no matter what I was doing, I was always disciplined, and that was what it took for me to be successful in this business. There are a lot of people who want a lot of things, but if you are not able to spend the time it takes, and continue pushing to reach that goal without giving up, it will be very hard to reach."

You have probably heard something similar in your life at some point, but coming from Anthony made it so profound. He made a great point—read this slowly—you need to be willing to *put the time and the effort in* to create the change that will enable you to reach the goal that you desire. I want you to realize that this is something that anyone can do. The definition of discipline is: "An activity, exercise, or a regimen that develops or improves a skill; training." Every day that you wake up you should say out loud "I am disciplined!" There will be many things I will have you saying aloud throughout this book, because making things known to yourself out loud is much more effective than just thinking it.

I am excited to help you grow!

Please write down your biggest take away

from this Chapter and reflect on it.

_____

—

_____

—

_____

—

_____

—

_____

—

_____

—

_____

—

_____

—

_____

—

_____

—

CHAPTER 2

CHOOSE TO BELIEVE YOU CAN

They say old dogs can't learn new tricks! Maybe so, but people can! I believe, no matter how old you are it is never too late to make a change in life, even if you are feeling stuck. I preach to my entrepreneurial students that they must always *believe* in themselves and have the *courage* to continue being *motivated to take action*.

And like each one of them, **YOU** have a significant purpose. Of course, it is ideal to start making great choices at a young age, early in your chosen career path. If so, you are way ahead of the game, and already going in the direction that you desire, instead of the opposite.

However, if this is not the case, and you feel like the old dog, don't despair, you can learn tricks to implement change to unleash your purpose and potential—as I begin to take you in a new direction. Read this carefully. I want you to digest these next thoughts. Nothing in life comes easy for anyone. There will always be challenges to overcome, but here is one very important thing I'd like you to understand that has value for you—*no matter how challenging the task, or the difficult experience of completing the task—your ability to overcome the obstacles within the challenge is priceless*. Sadly, some people never understand the value of overcoming obstacles to achieve what they set out to do.

You may be thinking to yourself—*Why not take the easy road, or why put so much work into a venture?* The reason people make the choice to be diligent, responsible and disciplined are because these things have a huge payoff—and they realize that they need to make them a lifelong habit if they are to succeed. It's all about having the right mindset, like I talked about in Chapter One, and making the commitment to yourself to be the best *you*, you can be! This takes work and sacrifice—clear goals and priorities—and in turn, you have to be willing to give up some things and make new choices in order to let the easy route diminish. It takes increasing your effort to go after the hard. It requires change and agreeing to accept the challenge. When working towards your goal, every day is stimulated with positive actions. Seriously, think how bored you would be if you snapped your fingers and got whatever you wanted, whenever you wanted. If you never had to work for anything in your life and always lived that way, you would feel extremely *unfulfilled*. It would be all too easy. You wouldn't grow as an individual or feel satisfaction, because you would have never discovered or accomplished anything difficult yourself.

This is not what you, me, or anyone else will take pride in or feel good about when we are older and reflecting back on our life. There is no other way to learn the value of this principle than to work hard—only then is the personal reward realized.

Another lesson that I learned, which is so simple, but easily forgotten, is to remember everything that we do in life is based on *choice*. Think about it. You have a choice when you cross the street at a specific time, you have a choice to talk to a stranger, you have a choice to take on another class, you have a choice to wake up and make things happen for yourself—every single day—and it is your choice on whether or not you achieve the life that you deserve to live. You have options and alternatives that you get to pick—and only you!

I am so passionate about this topic, because I believe in people—I believe in you! I KNOW without a doubt that everyone has the potential to do it—to live out their chosen passion and purpose. It kills me, inside, when I see someone who has so much going for them and they throw away their gift one day after another, because, for whatever reason, they just can't seem to carry out the actions that utilize their passion and skills. Don't let this be you. Don't let life pass by you without taking action. You have too much to offer this world and only **YOU** can tell yourself that you can't.

The saddest aspect of this situation is that I can understand why people have setbacks. I empathize with people who have unfortunate circumstances. I know that many people strongly desire to change their life. But it takes more than desire and thought; it takes motivation and action to create an outcome.

The place that I know best—and the place I need to take you—is to face your individual truth. The truth allows you to understand what makes certain situations difficult. It helps you see your specific circumstances, and commit to what has to be done to achieve realistic outcomes.

In order to create a direction and set your course, you must first understand where you are in your life. There is the starting block, and you "run the race"and progress from that starting point. I can give you all of the steps you need to take, and all of the tools to implement them, but if there is no *consistent action,* then there is no goal attained, no dream accomplished. When an individual fails to do this, it breaks my heart, because it comes down to belief in yourself—*that you can!* It requires belief in yourself—enough to step out on that track and get in the race! No one else can do that for you; you know it's true. So, I encourage you to courageously take that next step; seriously go after the challenge to get in the race; go after the life of your dreams!

I want you to know that I am rooting for you on the sidelines like a crazy cheerleader screaming at the top of my lungs yelling, "You can do it!"

I plead with you not to take this book lightly, and the actions it guides you towards. It's here to help you. If you put in the hard work, you will create an amazing future for yourself. Now that I am all riled up, let's start

by thinking about where you are headed
now. . .

What direction are you headed?

What are you currently doing for a job, school
or career? (Please explain in a few sentences.)
Write from your heart, and <u>describe where
you want to head</u>. Be candid; it may not even
sound so good, right now, but change is on its
way. Be real and honest with yourself. The
more information you provide, the better off
you will be in terms of taking action to create
positive changes, and meet your specific
goals. There is no right or wrong answer here,
only to be completely honest with yourself.
When I was young, I had no idea where I
wanted to go or what I wanted to do after I
graduated, so if someone had asked me this
question then, I would have been dumbfound-
ed. But I knew I wanted to help people, and I
wanted to change lives, so even recognizing
that much was a start. The good news is that
it doesn't have to be that same way for you. I
want to encourage you wherever you are in
life, and whatever your age, to write down
your thoughts and identify some ideas about
<u>where you see yourself</u>, and <u>what you would
like to do</u> going forward.

This is your new direction statement—I want to see you turn it from merely a dream to a reality for your life. Write it, believing, "Yes, I can!" (Please use a notebook if you need more room to write.) "Turn your dreams into doing!"

_____

_____

_____

_____

_____

_____

_____

_____

_____

_____

_____

_____

_____

_____

_____

_____

_____

_____

_____

CHAPTER 3

HAPPY WITH WHERE
YOU ARE HEADING?

You can let go of restricting habits that are hindering your success, and replace them with proven steps that will move you forward to live out your potential and purpose. No matter what circumstance you are in today, you can take on a positive mindset and a fresh belief in your abilities. As you further accept that you do have control over the choices you make, I will challenge you to think differently than you ever have before; this opens up your mind to new possibilities of what could be a possibility, or in store for your life. These things allow you to project more clearly where you are heading—and once you put it into action, you will be in a new place of mind *and* body.

Now, please answer the following questions with openness and honesty. Circle the an-

swers to each.

Are you happy with your current circumstances in your home environment? Yes   No

Do you currently have a job or career?   Yes   No

Are you happy with your decision in a career? Yes   No

Would you consider yourself on the right track in your personal life? Yes   No

Would you consider yourself on the right track in life professionally? Yes   No

Do you see yourself staying in your job or career? Yes   No

Are you ready to attack all challenges that come your way? (Such as. . . overcoming setbacks, having the right attitude when things get tough, making tough decisions with confidence, etc.) Yes   No

Do you watch television less than one hour a day? Yes   No

Would you say that you are open to change? Yes   No

On a daily basis do you consider yourself to be productive? Yes   No

Do you feel you are an innovative thinker? Do you think freely? Yes   No

Do you desire to be GREAT? Yes   No

Do you feel that you currently have an "Action Plan" for your life personally? Yes   No

Do you feel that you currently have an "Action Plan" for your life professionally? Yes   No

At this point in time, do you see yourself as a successful individual both personally and professionally? Yes   No

These questions are a great way to evaluate your current mindset and your personal thoughts about your life. If you answered "yes" to most of them, then you are feeling confident about the direction you are headed. Of course, that's really encouraging and good!

If you answered "no" to many of them, then you may have some confusion and/or lack of purpose. Those areas require careful thought and planning, and change and action to bring clarity and positive results. Keep them in mind as you proceed through this book. It will help you prepare as you choose to take action in a specific direction.

Back to your ability to choose—think about it like this—consider two scenarios.

You are standing in front of a massive forest and there is only one way to get to the other side— you must make your way through it. You have not prepared as you should have, and you don't have a flashlight, shovel, tent, food, or anything that you will need for survival. You have no idea how long you will be in this forest, and because you did not take any tools or prepare yourself, it will be difficult, maybe even impossible, to get to the other side.

On the other hand, if you were prepared with the tools and the mindset to know where you were headed, got a map and studied it, the chances of you getting to that other side would be much more realistic. Think about how confident you would feel, and how prepared you would be if you had food to eat, a tent to sleep in, and a gun for protection. You would feel good; you would feel less anxious and secure, because you were prepared.

Preparation is so important regardless of what it is you are prepping for in life, because you never know when you need to count on your mindset, your organization, and your tools for survival.

I've used this example to remind you that there are always obstacles to face in most everything you do, so whenever possible, I highly recommend doing whatever you can to be prepared for them. Take advantage of shared wisdom, and apply it to the opportunities that are presented to you. If someone recommends you to go to an educational workshop—sign up and go. If you are presented the opportunity to meet someone in your field who has a successful track record—take advantage of learning from that person. If someone is willing to give you advice, because they have been there and they understand your situation—listen and learn. Be open-minded and aware of what is going on around you, being ready to receive whatever might be right in front of you—that will benefit you!

What do you feel are the most important personal tools you need to have when going through life's challenges? Think of this both personally and professionally. Look at your life in its entirety and please share your specific thoughts.

There are no right or wrong answers here.

Tools are things that are utilized positively in your life, and may be tangible to others, or may only be known by you. They may be a natural gifting that comes easily, taught skills, or personality strengths.

_____
_____
_____
_____
_____
_____
_____
_____
_____
_____
_____
_____
_____

I am always anxious to see what people say when I ask them about their "personal toolbox," because each individual has their own ideas of what are great tools and what aren't. And different goals demand that we adapt to a variety of requirements and adopt specific skills that pertain to those goals. We all work differently to achieve our desired end result, so what works for one individual may not for another. That's where your personal tools and gifts come into play!

In a few brief sentences tell me how you are working towards your dreams and ambitions at this point in your life. What tools are you currently using to make your dreams a reality?

For example, please provide action items that are moving you forward, or people that are helping you to be accountable, such as a coach you are working with, etc. (Working with a coach is one of the best ways to stay consistent with what you are trying to accomplish. They help you create an effective strategic life plan for your overall vision— helping you to achieve what you desire. After working with many clients, I can attest to results that are attained much quicker, due to the accountability factor.)

_____

_____

_____

_____

_____

_____

_____

_____

_____

_____

_____

_____

_____

If you are not sure where you are headed in life, then know that you are surrounded by millions of others who feel the same way. It is an extremely difficult decision to make a commitment to one career path for the rest of your life. I don't want you to think that you need to make that decision right now. We live in a time in history where everything is evolving faster than we ever imagined. Everywhere you look changes are being implemented through education, technology, business, etc. **The important thing for you to remember is that <u>it is always better to do something than nothing at all</u>.** To remain stagnant and not do anything will diminish your ability to grow and achieve realistic goals. I personally believe there are so many choices thrown at us all at once when we are entering the work force or in life period, that it makes it nearly impossible to make a decision to pick just one career path and to make those life-altering decisions. It's kind of like when you have been to the grocery store when you are hungry. You walk down the aisles and want literally everything on the shelves, because there are so many yummy options, and all your stomach can think about is food!

Like me, I'm sure you've done this. I've gone to the grocery store when I was absolutely starving, and before I knew it my entire cart was full of junk. I wasn't sure what I wanted, but I knew I was extremely hungry.

We are often distracted from what is good for us. In this scenario, what I really needed was healthy food which nourished my body, but instead was tempted by all of these other goodies.

You can look at all of the distractions in your life in a very similar fashion. You should be moving toward your calling, and try not to be tempted to engage in activities, careers, and lifestyles that are not moving you toward becoming your best you. Try to avoid the junk!

Whether or not you realize where you are trying to go, all of us have an innate intuition inside—where you can ask yourself if you feel right about your involvement in your current situation—and it's a trusted gauge. **Ask yourself, when you are involved in something, "Is this good for me, and really what makes me happy and brings me fulfillment?"** You will get an immediate answer—through feeling a sense of accomplishment or an unsettled dissatisfaction. Asking yourself that question, will make a world of difference in your mindful decision-making process. There are many people who say, "I know what I want to do, but I am not sure how to get there," then there are others who feel as if they have no direction at all. Ask yourself, "Which am I?"

Confusion can be a very good thing, let me tell you why. Confusion can evoke new thoughts and innovative ideas. It can wake you up to reality and help you make decisions based on current and past experience. At the very least, if you are confused you are looking for fresh options and new direction.

I used to work at a college, as an admissions director, and would take call after call from individuals who were trying to discover their life purpose. They were from every facet of life. Some were very young, just out of high school; some of them were older than my parents, and had lost their jobs and were looking to work toward a new direction. It was devastating to hear all of their stories of job loss, cutbacks and layoffs. Of course you can't predict exactly where life will take you, and there will always be unexpected occurrences that take place, but no one can take from you the solid base of dreams you desire in your heart—and the hope you have to accomplish them, so that you can live a fulfilling life.

I personally believe that we are put in a place for a period of time to do something significant, and when that time is over that chapter closes, and another door opens. All experiences contribute to what you know and who you are today. And no matter what direction you choose in life, there are always going to be tribulations and hardships, as you have probably already realized, but that does not mean you cannot overcome them. We all go through challenges that will test us. *Will we persevere? How do we persevere?*

For me personally, I rely on God to help me persevere, so that I can live my dream of coaching others how to achieve their dreams. My purpose is to help you accomplish a purpose driven life, the absolute maximum you can imagine for yourself, *to become the best you can be!* You will achieve whatever you set out to do if you follow your heart's desires, get in the race and stay in the race, by putting what you know into action. And even when circumstances make it hard—always remember to believe in yourself, even if what you are trying to accomplish seems impossible! You are special and significant, and have much to offer this world—more than you can ever imagine as you may feel right now, as you read this today. Be proud of the potential that awaits you.

Remember, there are many mountains that we have to climb before our life comes to an end. Sometimes we will feel on top of a sunny mountain, other times we will feel in a dark and foggy valley. Life will continue to be a journey, regardless of the position we are standing in.

In order to continue persevering, and climbing to the top of the next mountain, you need to follow through by holding your head up high. Your inner strength to move forward is based on your ability to believe in your potential.

What would it take to climb that mountain?

I am sure you have heard someone say, "He is going nowhere fast," or "She is going in a downward spiral." These are quotes associated with individuals who have no direction. Anyone can fall into these categories, because direction setting can be a challenge, but for everything in life there are systems and strategies that can be followed. No matter where you are going or what you are trying to attain, there is always a way to do it.

Right now, I want you to make a conscious decision. Tell yourself, out loud, that you are ready to make your dreams a reality!

My mother used to say to me as a child, *"Where there is a will, there is a way!"* I have stood by this quote my entire life. Fortunately, regardless of where you are in your life, even if you feel you are headed in the wrong direction, you will be able to change the sails and make a shift. And for others, even though you think you are going in the right direction, you may be so unclear about how to get there, that you haven't really made any of the *key* steps that are necessary to achieve results.

You can add a million tasks to your list of ambitions you would like to achieve, but until you start crossing them off your "to do" list, you will continue to remain stagnant in your current circumstances. It may be that you need to figure out the "how" before you take any kind of action. The "how" creates clarity in your mind, and is usually the hardest part to determine when achieving goals. We have been going over some very important information so I hope that you are thoroughly engaged. I want you to know that each and every successful person has a *starting point* and a *struggle*. Life is frustrating, but fabulously exciting at the same time.

You need to know, I get down too. And when I get down about a situation, I think of all of the people that are going to benefit from the products and services I am creating. (Believe me, it's hard work, and a progression of good and bad events, over several years, to have anything worthwhile to create or write in a book!)

I remind myself how honored I am to change people's lives by giving back in every way that I possibly can. *Your success brings me fulfillment.* Therefore, if I get setback which we all do from time to time, I get right back on my feet and keep on going, because I don't want to let you or anyone else down that could potentially benefit from what I want to share! I've seen how others achieve results from what I offer. Watch for the same in your life.

Let's get right to it!

I want to start off by asking you, "Do you have short and long term goals at this

point?" My goal is to make sure that you are very clear on EXACTLY what you want out of your life. I want you to begin brainstorming about what it is you are most passionate about. Whether you have a love for the arts, business, education, etc.— I want you to think about how that specific passion can be incorporated into your life. Also, think about if you already have an involvement with your passion. If you do, let's gear it up to a whole new level!

Using the following exercise, I want you to think creatively "outside the box." Imagine what would make you most happy and bring out your utmost passions. <u>Write down five sentences that describe your passion and/or ambitions</u>. This is a great way to look at yourself from an outside standpoint and begin a personal evaluation. I want you to really think about this, because whether you are going into a different field, starting a new career, or making a personal change, it is important to understand as much about yourself as you can. It will also help you make better choices based on what you sincerely desire for your future.

Going forward, please try to be as specific as possible about these **ambitions (goals and**

hopes) and **passions (zeal, enthusiasm and purpose).** Brainstorm where your ambition and passion can take you. What doors of opportunity do you hope will open? Why does it matter to you? Here's an example, "I love to sit down at a baby grand piano and play classical music for hours, because the act of making music brings me joy."

Now, you give it a shot. Describe your passions and/or your ambitions:

1._____

_____

_____

_____

_____

_____

_____

2._____

_____

_____

_____

_____

_____

_____

3._____

_____

_____

_____

_____

_____

_____

4._____

_____

_____

_____

_____

_____

5._____

_____

_____

_____

_____

_____

Did you further realize your potential—simply by writing down what you are passionate about? It just needs to be tapped into. We are really getting into some good stuff now! YOU! I am sure you have great ideas about what you would like to accomplish in life, and my job as your accountability coach is to encourage and motivate you to put the plan and action behind it to help you make it happen.

If you feel that you have come to a cross-road and are confused, you are feeling what most people experience at some point in their life. I look at crossroads as a good thing because you only have two options. Most of the time, one of the options is to seize the opportunity for change—and the second option is to accept right where you are and stay just the same. This by no means suggests that making a crossroads decision is easy. Crossroad decisions are among the hardest in life. In my personal experience with crossroads, I have always taken the route of opportunity and change, because I have realized that in order for me to achieve what I really wanted out of life, I needed to give some things up.

First, I had to know what I wanted—and that's what I want you to consciously recognize today. Whether it is ending a relationship, moving to a new state, leaving a job, or whatever the case may be, **you will be giving up *something* in order to receive something new.** Think about this for a second. Each thing that I just mentioned can be looked at as a risk, but can also be perceived as an opportunity. And I can tell you from personal experience that I gave up all three of these at different crossroads in my life. Every time I trusted my heart and let go, I was able to move forward with more power and confidence than the previous crossroad. **Each time you pursue opportunities for positive change, you will receive experience and possibilities that you likely haven't received before.** I cannot begin to tell you all of the wonderful things that have happened to me as a result of letting go of my fears, and stepping up to create change.

What about age?

Many people think that the younger you are, the harder it is to envision your future. I feel that any age has its challenges and frustrations, but it is never too early or late to start making a concrete plan of action.

I am so excited you are reading this, because after implementing these strategies you are going to excel faster than you ever imagined. Alright—get ready to move forward! I need to make this very clear—when it comes to goal setting, you will be moving toward a chosen destination point. However, I never want you to think you have completely reached the pinnacle of your life ambitions. I know this sounds a little bit crazy, but if you reach the top of what you think you should achieve and have everything that you ever wanted, then what? What do you have to look forward to?

In short, accept the fact that you will always be a work in progress. There's always more! You will still want to attain new goals, and be consistently growing. The need and want to grow continues to evolve as we go through life, since personal growth is what gives our day its purpose. We all grow in different ways and at different speeds. You are completely unique, and so is your growth cycle.

I encourage you to have a mindset, and create a lifestyle where you are incorporating growth ALL the time! How cool is that if you are able to feel accomplished every single day of your life? Imagine how it feels to live a life of fulfillment, purpose, increased awareness and consciousness. Potential and opportunities await you, and it's such an honor to help you realize that through writing this book.

The first seven steps that need to take place starting NOW! These are things that you absolutely must create for yourself. Let me say it one more time! *These are things that you absolutely must create for yourself!*

> **The time is now,**
>
> **I might not know how,**
>
> **Buts that's ok,**
>
> **I can start today.**
>
> **No matter what—I will find a way!**

This is called the jump start poem to memorize. It helps to keep you motivated to accomplish daily tasks! Write it down; remember it. Now, let's keep moving forward.

SEVEN ACTION STEPS TO ACHIEVE HOW YOU BEGIN TO GET IN THE RACE

Action Step #1

Create a Vision Board.Picture your ideal life!

You'll need:

- a poster board
- a stack of old magazines
- stickers
- scissors
- markers
- glue or tape

This vision board should be full of pictures, words, and statements! The pictures should be images of things you strongly desire to have in life. We, as human beings, have a photographic memory, so seeing this everyday will insert subconscious thoughts of achieving and succeeding in your mind.

For written statements, make statements as if you have already attained them, such as, "I lost twenty pounds and I look awesome!" or "It feels good to have a million dollars in my bank account!" Also, a subconscious entity that some don't think about is putting an exclamation point at the end of a sentence to give that belief statement extra energy!

I encourage you to make your board beautiful, unique and fun! Get excited about doing this, knowing that it really is going to make a difference in your life! Then, take the time to make it happen, if you don't take the time to do this for yourself, no one else will! This is one more step in the right direction. A vision board is also something that you can do with a group, which makes it lots of fun! Speaking from experience, I can say that creating one with a group is a blast, because all the while each person is chatting, suddenly creativity flows and the boards come to life! Your vision board is so unique; you learn about what is important to you, and if doing it with others—

them, too!

Your vision board reminds you daily of what you are working towards. Things to put on the vision board consist of:

- Pictures that excite you

- The goals you are working toward

- Quotes or scripture that inspire you

- Images that remind you of what you desire to achieve

- People you would like to do business with, or have as mentors

- Places you would like to travel; purchase

- Anything that can be put on it to bring you positivity, motivation, and encouragement, to help you move towards your goals

Action Step #2

Do not multitask!

Focus on one thing at a time. I cannot stress this enough and I'll tell you why. *When you try to do too many things at once unfortunately nothing ever gets done well.* I know this can be frustrating, because you have so many important tasks that need completion. Here is the catch, you can start ten projects and have good intentions of getting them all accomplished, but it will take you forever to achieve finalization of even one of them. You will be going back and forth trying to do everything for each one and it will make you insane. This is one of my greatest, personal challenges. I have had many experiences trying to take on multiple projects at once, and it is incredibly difficult. It will be much easier if you allow yourself to concentrate on one task at a time. Make sure you focus on that task, bring it to a close, complete it to the best of your ability and then start on the next one.

Action Step #3

Prioritize!

Organize according to importance. Make a list of all of the things that you need to do every day and ask yourself, "What are the top three things on my list that have the most importance?" When I say importance, remember, *importance signifies priority.* They should be tasks that are going to help you achieve closer status to achieving your goals and living your passion and purpose.

Achieving one goal at a time ensures you will accomplish your tasks, which boosts your confidence. Make sure to implement everything you do in accordance to their importance, or you are setting yourself up for failure! Work towards completing your number one task, without deviating to other tasks that are not as important. It may take a little bit of time if you are used to doing a million things at once, but in order <u>to achieve the goals that you want in life</u>, do *more* with *less*.

Action Step #4

Simplicity is the Key!

If you simplify things, you make life easier for yourself and others, because you understand exactly what steps you should take. For example, you wouldn't look twice at a book that recommends using one thousand steps to help you create your ultimate purpose. It's too complicated. But you would opt for a book that has a "seven step method," because it gives you a simple, doable way to attain your goals. .

Make your life simple where you can, because

it will allow you to appear clear to others and to yourself—and you will be able to get your point across, without confusion. Think about how this works in any situation, whether it involves relationships, business, everyday communications, etc. **Don't** make your life harder than it needs to be. If there is a way to accomplish tasks in an easier manner, but still create the same results in what you would like to achieve, then take advantage of that system.

Action Step #5

Clarity is a must!

Clarity gives your life direction and allows you to map out a specific pathway to get there. This will also allow you to smooth off the rough edges of areas in your life that cause confusion. Let's take goal setting for example. Pretend you decided you wanted to go and attain a Master's degree, and you weren't sure when or how you were going to do it. You just decided one day that you would like to go back and receive that amazing degree. Well, this is a great, ambitious goal, but if there is no conscious rhyme or reason to it, people un-fortunately would not succeed. The goal is too generalized. To create a clear vision, you need to be as specific as possible about "why" you want to do it, because when you are specific you are able to develop motivation and an attachment to that goal. In turn, you create deadlines for yourself that hold you accountable.

To create personalized goals for yourself, the key is to be specific, realistic, and create a timeline for each one to be completed. This way, you can successfully implement them on a day-to-day basis. Goal setting can seem daunting, but with renewed clarity your vision is better defined, and therefore easier to identify how steps will be taken.

Action Step #6

Time is of the essence!!

You only have a precise amount of time on this earth, so you must utilize it wisely. It is necessary to have strong time management skills. Even if you are struggling with time management, it is a skill that can be learned and implemented. Lifestyle changes and learning new skills can take time, but once you get them down, you will conquer one goal after another. You should be able to prioritize the things in the order of importance of what you ultimately want accomplished—and learn to say no to yourself and others when it does not help you move towards your purpose. Doing things, such as, sitting in front of the television, or playing video games will not get you any closer to your goals. Once again, the real question is this, "What are the most important things that you want to achieve with your life?" If you have a passion for something but you are not doing it, then can I ask you "WHY NOT?" Is there time that is being wasted that could be better utilized?

Action Step #7

Seek out your passion

You have the potential to be involved in anything that you seek. Have you ever heard the saying, "Those who seek shall find and the door shall be opened for them?" You need to sit down and think about all of the attributes that you possess, and then reflect on them to formulate your passion—up close and personal. *Once you can perceive in your mind exactly what you are seeking to find, this naturally initiates a direction, and through that direction you will develop a plan and purpose.* For some, this can be quite difficult, because many people are passionate about a broad variety of things. To seek out your ultimate purpose, you need to delve deep into your soul and answer a few questions:

Who do I believe myself to be?

_____

_____

_____

_____

_____

_____

_____

_____

_____

In what ways do I contribute (or desire to contribute) to humanity? Why does it have value?

_____

_____

_____

_____

_____

_____

_____

_____

To whom do I hold myself accountable? (To what am I held accountable? For example: family, coach, spouse, fellow students, etc. Why are you held accountable to them, or he/ she?)

_____
_____
_____
_____
_____
_____
_____
_____

When do I feel most fulfilled?

_____
_____
_____
_____
_____
_____
_____
_____

These are all questions that you need to answer in order to develop a passion for *your purpose*. Passion is the adrenaline that pushes you toward getting off to a great start! I want you to look back on this chapter and recognize how far you have come in such a short period of time. A plan is starting to take form, to get you well on your way to creating a strong and exciting path for your future.

What is at least one take away from this chapter that you will start implementing to-day? What steps (from above) are you are will-ing to implement in order to work toward your first goal?

CHAPTER 4

NEVER GIVE UP, EVER!

Is this true for you? A fear of success—and along with that, a fear of change! If this is you, I want to help you get over your fear, because there is a vast amount of your potential waiting to be claimed—through a type of businesses, career, or life ambition—let's get a move on and take action together! You must be willing to "go for it"!

Well. . . the question that you have to ask yourself is "What do you fear?" I'm not talking about a life-threatening type of fear that is critical to your well being; I'm talking about *imagined* fears. Pinpointing these types of fears is crucial, because they stop your progress dead in your tracks. Of course, if we had no fear of anything, we would do whatever we wanted without worry or concern, so some fear is good for us. However, one of the biggest fears that we all possess is failure, but we cannot look at it as a negative thing. Instead, it needs to be embraced, because at one point or another, and whether we like it or not, we are going to fail.

Learning to look forward to failure can be an awkward thought, but if you look at failure as something positive versus something negative, it can completely change your outlook on life. You will be unstoppable, because fear of failure no longer invades your thoughts as being a bad thing. The *great thing* about failure is the lessons you will learn from it.

I have failed many times in my life, and I have tried numerous businesses that turned out to be a total disaster. I'll tell you about one. When I was twenty-one years old, I had the bright idea to start my own dog clothing company by the name of, "My Sexy Dog." I thought it was the greatest name in the world for a dog shop, and I felt dog owners would love it. After all, who doesn't think their dog is sexy, right? Well, at least I did! But as I shopped for sexy, classy, fun fabrics, I learned they were expensive! How could I possibly afford all of this? So, I did what any other new business owner does, put it on my credit card!

I took the fabric home and began to implement my plan—and started to create the most sophisticated dog clothes on the market. It was really exciting imagining little dogs running around wearing "My Sexy Dog." I planned to price on the expensive side, and use high end materials only. Don't laugh, but because *I didn't have a clue about sewing*, I thought that I would hire a seamstress to do the sewing for me. I hired a woman who was artistic and very creative; the only problem was that she was charging me $12.00 an hour. To make matters worse, she was only able to make one article of clothing per hour. Costs were adding up quickly. I decided I would look for another seamstress, because my plan was to launch the clothing line at a fashion show in about a month, which I was planning to host in downtown Chicago. I was so excited about it!

After some thorough research, I managed to find another seamstress who lived in the neighboring town. I dropped the rest of my material over to her. I thought I was in a great situation, because I had two women working on my creations who were very well known for their seamstress work. I developed the designs, and they were able to sew the material together. With all of the wonderful people I had working with me to increase exposure and promotion, I was sure that the event would be a success! As the event neared, I called the woman from the neighboring town on multiple occasions to see how the clothes were turning out. There was no answer! I must have called about thirty times to get in touch with her, and still no answer. Not only did she have my original designs and fabric, but my sexy doggy designs needed to be completed by the next week. I was freaking out! Two days before, I finally managed to reach her, and to my horror she had done *nothing* to create the clothes. I was devastated. She said she was terribly sorry, but just could not figure out how to do it. I could not believe she didn't call me and tell me so I could get someone else. At least, I had some designs created by the other woman, so it was better than nothing.

On the day of the show, I arrived early, and brought the clothes that were completed for the show. I scurried around to be sure everything was set and ready to go. It got closer to showtime, and another of my *worst fears* came to pass—none of my dog "models" were there to wear the clothes. Of the five different people I'd asked to bring in their dogs—not one showed up. I couldn't believe it! People began to sit down, and I knew there was no way I could pull this off, because I had no models except my own dog. In an absolute panic, with my little Chihuahua, Sparky, I ran out of there crying in desperation and embarrassment. I sat in my car for a few minutes, and I realized that I had humiliatingly failed. I knew that even though the circumstances were not my fault, I still was responsible. I was devastated from the experience. I wanted it to be a success, but unfortunately things don't always play out as we desire or expect them to.

From this disastrous venture, I learned how important it is to have a backup plan, especially when you have put so much time and effort into an endeavor. I continued to work on "My Sexy Dog" for quite a while, but realized it wasn't enough for me to spend my life selling dog clothes; I wanted to change people's lives. This process helped me to learn another great life lesson and it's this: It's not until we actually try something that we find out if it is truly our passion and life ambition. It's true, that at the time we experience a heartbreaking event, it can seem that it is the worst thing that has ever happened. I have come to believe, however, everything happens for a reason and there is always a lesson to be learned—from any failure. Believe me, seldom are we limited to only one failure in life, unless we never try again. Remember that your dreams don't expire, so get a good night's sleep, wake up refreshed tomorrow and try again.

Let others inspire you. . .

I will never forget my freshman year in high school at a State Conference in track; I witnessed one of them most breathtaking moments in my life. Becky Wiseman, a senior at the time, was a track star on our team and she was an incredible runner. She had run all four years, and managed to perform amazingly well, improving her times every year. But there was one thing that Becky hadn't done, and that was to beat her competition from Sterling. Sterling was by far our biggest competitor, and it was a constant rivalry in every sport! Not surprisingly, Becky made it past the first two heats into the finals in the 200

meter dash. Before the final she realized she would be running against the girl from Sterling, whom she had never beaten, and this would be her last chance.   I went up to wish her good luck right before the final was called, and she said, "Genesis, I am going to WIN!" I looked at her intently and knew she was right. I could see it in her eyes. There was a sparkle of faith and confidence. Pure determination accompanied her to the starting line. I watched as she walked over to the blocks with a fierce ambition to win. She had made a decision before she stepped into those blocks that she was going to cross that finish line in first place! There was a great silence that fell over the crowd waiting for all the runners to take off. I could barely breathe as I saw them all step into the blocks. I wanted her to win so badly, and this was her last chance as a senior to win the conference title.

All of a sudden, the shot rang out and they were off. The crowd went into a screaming frenzy, with each section cheering on their own team. I screamed "Come on Becky you can do it, this is it, your last chance!" Down the 100 she came, neck and neck with the Sterling girl who she so desperately wanted to beat. Only 50 meters to go, Becky and the Sterling girl pulled ahead of the others. This was going to be a photo finish! Only 10 meters left and it was a matter of pure will for whoever was going to give it their all to pull ahead. Becky sped into action, and for the last five meters lunged forward throwing herself over the line—and she did it! *She did it!* She won conference! She made it happen! The crowd was screaming and yelling, and it was almost as though time stood still, because the moment was so significant for her and the team. I love to tell this story, because it is one of my favorites of someone who wanted something so badly that she was were willing to do anything within her power to get it. I was proud to be her friend and teammate. It is experiences like this that show you can accomplish anything if you never give up running with all you've got, right through to that very last meter.

I have come to you today with the intention of pushing your mindset forward to a place that it has never been before. I want you to know that in any difficult situation, your thinking may automatically tend to take the easy route, the one of least resistance—which is to give up and quit. There are no quitters as far as I am concerned, and I will not allow YOU to be one. I will do everything in my power to keep you moving forward to take action, because it is when you stop and become distracted that you veer off course. Do not submit to anything, but remain focused on your goal. Your main desire in life should be to live for your purpose.

I want you to think about all of the things that you have experienced in your life up until this point, *and list for me an experience in which you were <u>not</u> willing to give up.* I know that you have gone through them, because at some point in your life you have come to a situation and said, "I am going to make it through this!" This can be correlated to any situation. What was yours? (This can be taking a test, running a race, taking care of a loved one, etc.)

_____

_____

_____

_____

_____

_____

_____

_____

_____

_____

_____

_____

Going forward, think about your current mindset, and again try to concentrate on your
strengths and not your weaknesses. No matter
how strong you are in an area you can always
get stronger. If you feel you are a confident
person, you can become more confident; if
you feel you are ambitious, you can be more
ambitious and so on and so forth.   Please list
ten positive qualities about your mindset. (For
example, persistent, realistic, humble, optimistic, vulnerable, no regrets, curious,
strategic, creative, etc.

1.

2.

3.

4.

5.

6

7.

8.

9.

10.

I hope that you didn't have to think too hard, because you have more positive qualities than you can ever fathom. As you grow into a more mature adult, you will realize that your mind-set, values, strengths, ambitions, motivations and goals will grow with you. This is the great thing about life, you are always learning because you are always experiencing. No one can take away your life experience, and the older you are the wiser you will become.

I am so proud that we are now in Chapter Four of *your new beginning in your life race*. There are many exciting things that you will learn about yourself yet to come.

In conclusion to Chapter Four, please write this: *"I will never be defeated because I am strong willed and confident; I will never ever give up!"* Then I want you to say it aloud.

Next, tell me why you will never be defeated as you challenge yourself to reach for the goal of your dreams. And who will help you make sure that you stay strong in this process? 😌

CHAPTER 5

GETTING TO KNOW
THE REAL YOU

Growing up, I never felt good enough. I share more about this later in this chapter, but I always felt there was something that I needed to prove to people. I wish it hadn't taken so long for me to get to know myself, because, like Aristotle once said, *knowing yourself is the beginning of wisdom*. So, if you haven't already, I want to encourage you to come face-to-face with the real you—it's never too early or ever too late. To do this, may require ripping off the mask, stop pretending, or to quit allowing yourself to be fake or phony to assure approval of certain groups of people or family members.

Whatever the label we place on ourselves, or our perception of our individual behaviors, the fact is—every individual is a blend of positive and negative traits. Not one of us is perfect, so it's best to accept that as an absolute truth about human nature, because that's you and me. Even though at times you may have chosen to copy what you see as acceptable choices and behaviors in others (we've all done it at one time or another)—it is time to stop—and to begin to appreciate you! Today, choose to approve of yourself, be happy, and let any setback you may have had serve to get you fired up to become your best, so you not only stay in the race, but achieve your potential.

Have you ever seen people act a certain way and you know that this is not who they truly are? As if they are fulfilling a role in a play, they are *pretending*. I observe this behavior in people all of the time, but the sad part is that I don't see it in just young adults; I see it in people of all ages. This false behavior denies who they truly are—and is an exterior façade. It is unfortunate, because if you or anyone else does not have a grasp on who they are as a person, and love themselves for their unique qualities, how can they, *or you*, possibly reach a destination point you would like to attain in life? Acting inconsistently with who you are, throws you every-which-way, and it is usually driven by how other people think you should act, feel or be. Once again, this is the time to stop the pretense or the wearing of a mask.

This is worthy of saying again: To unleash your potential, you cannot go through life without a clear understanding of your *true identity*, potential and purpose. Life causes all of us to be forced into dealing with one situation after another, but if you have a strong foundation of who you know yourself to be, and what you want out of life, you will not become defeated or hopeless dealing with challenges. Instead, you will have direction in your life, even if it sometimes requires changing direction to be true to yourself. Knowing yourself and your chosen purpose will help you pursue the right career, choose compatible relationships, and make right and thoughtful decisions to further your success. It can be hard to face, but if you are not making choices based on who you truly are, you can become frightfully lost and alone.

Young adults need to ask themselves, "What is my true identity?" Only then will they be able to place themselves on the right track. And if you are an older adult, and if you didn't find the right path earlier, it's never too late to "get to know the real you!"

I want to help you begin to evaluate your personality starting now—let's celebrate the real you! Begin taking notes about yourself. Going forward, I want you to use a notepad or iPad, something that allows you to make candid references about yourself in specific circumstances. (Examples: happy, sad, insecure, anxious, confident, angry, frustrated, inspired, motivated, creative, passionate, etc.)

When you look at yourself, what do you feel most strongly? Do you have a strong sense of contentment and peace regarding your life right now?   Or, are you insecure, depressed, sad, angry, or confused?

Below, I would like

you to share what feelings you typically experience when you look at yourself in the mirror, and then write why you think that is? It is important to highlight your emotions so that you can better identify any blocks that may be holding you back from doing your life's most desired and greatest work.

_____
_____
_____
_____
_____
_____

_____ Practice: <u>What does today's positive experience make you feel about yourself and your life</u>? I want you to mentally do this every day with at least one type of positive experience that you enjoy. How does this make you feel about yourself? Get in the habit of thinking about and enjoying your positive emotions.

Next, please share the five types of experiences you engage in on a daily basis that distract from future success, or do not enhance your feelings about yourself and/or your life. Next to each one, provide an emotion or feeling that the experience cre-

ates within you.

Such as:

Work – feeling bored and unfulfilled

Hanging with friends – risky and distracting

Social media – waste of time; feel inadequate

1.

2.

3.

4.

5.

This insight will help you to better understand yourself so that you can move away from jobs, people or activities that are preventing you from your ultimate progress and success.

In your journal or notebook, please write a summary of your day. Write what impact different experiences had on you; how they made you feel; how you reacted to them:

- An experience you enjoyed.

- An experience that created a better understanding of your unique nature.

- Time spent with family or friends; activities with them.

- An experience (work, hobby) that was stretching and fulfilling today. Why? What does it do for you?

- An experience that motivates you to want to learn more or spend more time doing it.

Do this for one month straight and you will begin to see your patterns of behavior, and learn an incredible amount about what makes you react (raising your awareness of both positive and negative experiences). This will begin to influence your choices and changes, and dreams and aspirations.

Proactive vs. Reactive Defined

To define—if you are **proactive**, you are ready before something happens; you prepare, anticipate and control a situation to the best of your ability.

<u>Being reactive is the opposite</u>—you wait for things to unfold before responding, enabling the person or stimulus to determine the outcome or experience. As you continue to read, you will learn whether you are *proactive* or

reactive. This is something very important to recognize in yourself. In this chapter you will be able to identify whether or not you are a proactive or reactive person on an average day.

Are You Proactive or Reactive (Circle A or B)

Question 1

A. You wake up early ready to take on the day with a "to do" list ready to go.

B. You like to take things at your leisure throughout the day.

Question 2

A. You have specific goals for your future with time lines attached to them.

B. You have goals, but they are generalized like "I would like to lose 30 pounds."

Question 3

A. You have a mindset that encourages you to take charge of every opportunity possible.

B. You feel that opportunities will come to you because if it is meant to happen *it will happen.*

Question 4

A. You desire to achieve more each day, growing, accomplishing, and developing.

B. You are satisfied with daily routine and feel that growth comes when it is the right time.

Question 5

1.You have a reason to wake up in the morning and try to achieve your daily goals/agenda.

1.You are very comfortable and dream a lot, but don't necessarily have a cause for your intentions on a daily basis.

If you answered mostly A's then you are considered a proactive person. You actively choose your destiny and don't expect things to happen to you. You make constant decisions and adjustments based on what you would like to achieve. People that are proactive tend to be happier due to the fact they are making their dreams a reality because they are constantly taking action.

If you answered mostly B's then you are a reactive person. You have reason to believe that your dreams will manifest themselves and that life just has a way of working itself out. You are waiting for life to happen to you. People that are reactive in their life tend to be more disappointed with life's outcomes.

I believe it is important for everyone to pursue being proactive. This does not mean you have to change your image or become someone who you are not. But being proactive allows you to take charge of your life! No one else has the authority to do that. And the payoff is—the more proactive you are, the more you can accomplish towards living out your potential on a daily basis—happily!

Many people, unfortunately, are reactive for their entire life and do not experience living out the dreams and ambitions that they wished to achieve. This is a choice that you will make every single day. Stay in your lane, don't veer off into another's lane, because you may end up being disqualified from your win—and your potential. Running another person's race will never get you far and will only cause you to stumble and you may end up right back at the starting line. *You can choose to make things happen, or you hang back and let things happen to you.* If you wait to let things happen to you, they just might not. Take control of yourself. Don't hesitate, make the right choice to go after your goals by continuing to move forward; be proactive by putting one foot in front of the other, consistently, day after day!

Awww. . . Confusion

It is difficult to determine who we are when we are confused. Confusion can come from many facets: unwanted forced change, multiple roles, too many choices, stage of life, others choices that influence ours, reality of life's circumstances, etc.

Sometimes there is no rhyme or reason to why we feel that way, other than we are in a more vulnerable season of life. It is important to realize that your confusion can create clarity in your mind, because it forces you to seek answers, draw fresh conclusions, and make difficult decisions.

Clearly, we live in a day and age where it is easy to get wrapped up in endless amounts of activities available to us. We have overwhelming options to infuse into our daily life. And opportunities, before and after graduation, and those that follow in life are many.

About forty years ago, it was different. The majority of women stayed home, did the housework and watched the kids, while the men worked outside the home. Society has changed so much. Now, both genders have equal opportunities for success in outside careers if they choose.

Please understand! We all have the ability to be great, whether we choose to work and mother in the home or pursue a career outside the home. There is no reason or excuse to believe otherwise.   Let's go through a few exercises so that you may evaluate yourself and make thorough determinations of your interests, perspectives and personal motivations. This will, in turn, create a strong sense of personal clarity and aid in helping you make solid decisions based on the belief system that you have already created for yourself. When you understand who you are, it creates confidence and endless amounts of opportunity for you to grow. People will gravitate toward you when they understand what you want to achieve in life. When you have a clear perception of what makes you special, you will exude your unique qualities and stand out from the pack.

So what is it that makes you different and special in your own way? Please think about it. There are so many things to consider: your personality, your unique gifts and skills, life experiences, your beliefs and perspective on life—or possibly your personal vision or dreams for your future.

Let's start by asking yourself about your personal interests:

- What kinds of events, social engagements, sports, etc. do you enjoy?

- What gifts or skills do you want to utilize in your career. At home?

- What do you believe that gives you strength and perspective in life?

- Where do you see yourself in five years?

- What three things do you value most in your life; things that are nonnegotiable.

- Who are the people that model who and what you hope to be like?

- Who is someone that could be a mentor in your life to you now, and how can you approach them about mentoring you?

These are all great questions to answer. This helps you commit time to doing the things you value. Pretending to be someone you're not, will stand in the way of your ultimate success. If you have a chameleon-like façade, it will only lead people to have a lack of trust in you. Inevitably, to be successful, you will have to go back to your true self, so why not be yourself to begin with—right now. The most significant part of being yourself, in my opinion, are the people who you start to draw towards you as you engage with all types of personalities. I have found that whatever type of attitude or personality you are portraying to others, you shall receive in return. Therefore, the more you are yourself, the more you will be surrounded by individuals who are like minded and living for similar purposes, with shared values. It is truly incredible to see how that works.

People who appreciate the beautiful and true you will start flocking into your life, and you will find yourself feeling that it is *so easy* to be yourself. It doesn't take all of the extra work that pretending to be someone or something else causes. *You are who you are*—accept you are not perfect, but know you have certain respected attributes. When you finally realize this by fully accepting the "real you,"

you will be able to completely walk away from all negative influences that are holding you back from pursuing your dreams. Suddenly, they become unimportant. Like in any relationship, boyfriends or girlfriends, best friends, associates—*whatever*—you should not have to work hard to fit in. Genuine people with whom you have a relationship will love you, for you, not for the person that *they expect* you to be. When it comes to true friends, I realize that good and faithful friends are few and far between, but it is worth it to hold out for the best, by giving your true best.

I also want to remind you of your associations with others, and how much of an impact even one person or multiple people you hang out with make in your life. Individuals who have the same mindset, or are respectful of differences, and are headed in a positive direction in their life. These types of people encourage you and me to be the best in our life. I recommend taking a frank look at your associations with others.

- Think about what kind of positive effect they have on your life.

- How are they helping you grow as an individual?

- What are they doing in life that you admire?

- How are they making a positive difference in their sphere of influence?

- <u>Or</u>, who are the people you can identify that are sucking all of the energy out of you? When thinking of them, the questions above can only be answered with a negative. (The stress or confusion you feel when you are with them is a good indicator.)

To know you is to love you! Ask:

- "How much do I really know about myself?" Would you answer that you have your values in line with who you are and what you want to do with your life?

- Do your values mesh well with the individuals you associate with?

- Do your words and actions represent what you believe when you go into the public eye?

- <u>Or</u>, do you shy away from the public eye because you don't want people to

see and know the real YOU (hidden behind a mask)?

By the end of this book you should better understand the real you. You should be able to
not look at your flaws, but concentrate on
your strengths. You will begin to live your life
to enjoy it, and work towards a career that
will bring you satisfaction, while utilizing
your potential. A pattern will emerge—a legacy is being built—that satisfies your yearning
to know that you are making a difference in
this world, day-by-day.

It all begins with understanding yourself,
your potential, your personality and your
purpose. I think that you will be pleasantly
surprised by the way that people (and not always the ones you expect) react to your positive actions as you further pursue your passion. They are attracted by ambition, motivation, love for the cause, and desire to help.

Today, how do you answer when others
ask you about your passion and motivation
regarding the goal you are pursuing or the
work that you do? What do you say? Do you
have a clear answer for them, or do you
question what your response should be?
Maybe you haven't thought about your passion
and motivations, but maybe you should. It's

all about you—*recognizing who you are as a person* helps you live your life to the fullest!

I may sound like you. . .

In the beginning of this chapter I mentioned that growing up I never felt I measured up to where I felt I should have been. I always felt there was something that I needed to prove to people. I believed that they would not accept me if I didn't act tough. I had the last name "Hey," and if you carried that name in my community, there was an expectation for me to behave a certain way. I guess you could say that I was a tomboy. I was raised around almost all boys, so I tried to live up to specific expectations. I never wanted to show any kind of weakness, because my personal self-confidence came from people recognizing me as being strong and confident and "good enough."

It was tough on my self-perception growing up a woman with so many men around. Little by little, throughout my life, I developed perfectionism, and began to have serious personal issues of self-acceptance. Everything that I did began to feel like a competition. I wanted to be the best in every single thing that crossed my path, but oddly enough,

I only discovered emptiness rather than satisfaction.

Everything became all about winning for me, and unfortunately no matter how many times I won it was never enough, and I was never fulfilled from the win, because it just pushed me to want to win more. Internally, I frequently felt defeated. It took a long time to recognize that winning is not everything and that losing can provide for a much better learning experience. Looking back it astonishes me to think I could have been so obsessed with a win vs. a loss. I do believe, however, it is important to give your all in every endeavor that you pursue, but when the focus becomes completely about yourself and satisfying your ego, you fall into trouble. That was me. I hadn't realized how bad it had gotten until I met a man at a training workshop, who is now a very dear friend of mine. After he asked me about myself, I explained to him in depth what I thought I should say, subconsciously not realizing I sounded almost desperate. I tried to explain to him all of the things I "thought" I should say. He looked at me and said "Genesis you are good enough."

Without even knowing me, he placed those words in my mind which I will never forget. I think he just sensed (from my desperate perfectionism) that those very words were the ones that I needed to hear. They resounded so strongly that I couldn't hold it together and started sobbing. I had built tremendous

pressure up within myself, and suddenly the dam burst. To hear *I was good enough*, just as I was, from a complete stranger made a significant impact. I realized from that moment on that it was not about my educational background, my expertise, or my personal circumstances that made up my self-worth. Suddenly, it hit me that I was good enough no matter what I had been through, no matter what my parents had or had not told me, no matter how much money I had, or what work I accomplished. Instead, I had an epiphany—within me; the key, the truth that turns the lock. ***What you believe yourself to be is who you will be.*** I want you to feel good enough to look into the mirror everyday and say "I am worthy to live a life of acceptance of myself! I am good enough!"

The acceptance board. You fit in here too!

In conclusion to Chapter Five, please write down what makes you unique, and helps you to positively stand out from other individuals? How do you define yourself as being special? Please say this aloud after you have written it down. This is just between "you and yourself," so acknowledge your strengths and attributes. It's time! ☺

_____

__

_____

__

CHAPTER 6

MISSION, VISION, VALUES

Your personal mission, vision, and values are of the utmost importance, and they point the way, stating the "why and what" of where you long to go in your life. These three significant determinants are beacons shining out in front of you, created from a yearning from deep within, defining and guiding you and your goals. They state on paper "who" you want to be as an individual. The only way to grasp future possibilities is if you know who you are, what you stand for and what you are passionate about—otherwise it is very difficult to know which direction to even head. Writing your mission and vision, and being clear about your values, is a great way to identify, and personally recognize, what makes you unique and special. These enable others to identify what makes you distinct, as well.

When someone can express their personal mission to me, I understand that they have a clear vision for their life; they know why there is a need in the world for what they want to do and they are ready to take the next steps toward accomplishing it.

Sharing with others your personal mission, vision and values can almost guarantee opening up doors of opportunity. I can't even begin to tell you how many times I have spoken to strangers about my personal mission and/or vision. They have grown into friends who have given me opportunities, or they have introduced me to someone else who was affiliated with my mission, or they helped me to make an awesome connection with a specific organization. These special opportunities would not have been granted to me if I had not been able to speak concisely and clearly about my personal mission and vision.

People can help you, too, if you allow yourself to be open to them. They can encourage and be messengers; they bring new confidence and connections to you in ways that will help you grow and prosper to achieve your ultimate potential. We are all interconnected to each other in one way or another, and being willing to open up to others reveals those connections. Connections are best started face-to-face, but I suggest you utilize all means possible to connect and stay connected with those who share your passion— through social media and Internet, phones and Skype, and other digital media outlets. It is truly incredible how you can move your vision forward if you take advantage of getting connected to others in every way possible. Let your passion shine through! The more passionate and genuine you are about your topic, the more drawn in people will be when you are communicating with them. And that is precisely why you need to develop these three things: Your personal mission, your vision and values.

When you are describing your personal mission in life, you may have many different types of ambitions and passions going through your mind. A mission is what you "live" for. My personal mission, to give you an example, is to help young adults and entrepreneurs create successful futures by helping them "get in the race and stay in the race," by tackling their goals one day at a time. I also provide an action plan and the tools they need to achieve the success they want.

I had to borrow a pair of boots from my cousin while visiting in Montana; as it turned out, the boots were about twice the size of my foot. Nonetheless, I persevered to climb with them! Sometimes your vision may seem too big for you too, but that doesn't mean it is too big for you to work toward. Always aspire to climb to the top!

Clearly, my passion is to help others achieve their dreams and their goals. Not only that, I would like to create a movement of reform for education that gives students opportunities to become entrepreneurs, helping them to develop into our leaders of tomorrow.

Your mission is yours—and entirely different, but what is it? Whether you are affecting people on a big scale or on a small scale, what you do makes a difference. The measure of success is measured one day and one person at a time—with hard work, in time, your mission will blossom.

Think about it. Are you an artist? Perhaps you love to play the piano and write music. Are you a sports fanatic? Maybe you would love to coach or teach. There are so many needs to fill in our world, so consider offering your skills to volunteer so you can gain experience in your chosen career path. The first step is to choose the direction you will go, at least for now. Expect to develop and change, and as you do so, so will your life choices.

Begin developing these by thinking about what makes you happy. Once you determine what brings you joy, it is much easier to correlate it with your passion, which is at the root of your vision. Recognizing this, naturally brings positive momentum, and becomes part of your makeup and mindset. Your enthusiasm and passion drives you onward as you move in a specific direction that keeps you focused on your mission.

Imagining this progression, next, I want you to write down five things that you are passionate about, with number one being what you are most passionate about, with number five being the least, but still, remember these are your top five.

1.

2.

3.

4.

5.

Now that you have determined your top five passions, you need to make them your active priorities. The order identifies where the heart of your passions lie. Were you surprised with the order? This activity shows you what is most important to you, and in doing so, it serves as the base, the very foundation of your personal mission statement for your life.

On the lines below I want you to consider those five things and write down your life mission. Don't worry; this isn't written in stone—it will flex and change. But it is the big picture that will ignite the process. *How can you promote something unique, and do it differently, because of the person you are? How will the world be a better place when your passions are put into play? What do you want to do, pursue or create, in regards to those five things you have prioritized and are passionate about?*

These may or may not change as time goes by, and do have to be frequently re-evaluated, but right now this will pull you into making decisions that line up with your passions and priorities, as you live your life today. This process of understanding what is important to you and what needs you can fill, helps you to move forward towards your vision for your future, and ultimately helps you unleash your potential. It's true that your success starts from within—now my hope is that you start to believe it!

_____

—

_____

A vision for your life is what you see, even when no one else can! It's how you see your future coming together. It brings energy to the mission statement and ignites the dream and motivates strategy of all the parts and pieces of where you see this going in one year, two years, three and more.

- Do you visualize yourself becoming a successful entrepreneur with your own small business?

- Do you see yourself running a national forest as the lead forest ranger?

- Could your vision be that you become the head of a corporation?

- Would you like to go back to school?

- Can you imagine yourself living the personal life you always have wanted to live?

- What are you making your life journey move toward? What is it? Why does it have value?

In order for you to have goals and dreams, you need to have a vision of what you want, and to be able to foresee how it will look as it plays out in your life; it's both as simple and complex as that. There are so many ideas and goals any one person can have, but as a coach my goal for you is to narrow everything down, so that it fits you to a "T." Allow yourself to develop your goals so that they are specific enough to make your vision turn into reality. I want you to succeed, and in order for you to do so, you will need to follow these instructional exercises as much as possible. The fact is—your vision for yourself is something that you will be working toward your entire life. A life vision is always bigger than you are! It is something that will never fully be met or ever die. It is a permanent part of who you are and what you long to do, and whom and what you hope to contribute and influence as you leave your mark on this earth.

Since learning and life experiences are ever-changing, you will never want to completely accomplish your life's work. I do not say this lightly, so don't let this statement confuse you. The point is—you never want to become stagnant or stop progressing. I have personally seen people floating through life with nothing to look forward to and I want to take them by the hand and open their eyes to all of the great possibilities that are staring them in the face. It is necessary to always be accomplishing something fresh and new—and to continue to grow and work toward something that is slightly out of reach. If you become stagnant, your purpose and drive will begin to dwindle, which causes a person to become nonproductive and bored with life. Growth comes with each challenging step, and you prosper and achieve your potential by continuing to move into higher and higher levels of challenge, life development and accomplishment.

Please take a minute to write down the vision that you see for your life, and remember that this vision does not have to be the same one that you have the rest of your life. Your vision will change and evolve just as you do as an individual. Keep in mind that this is an exercise for today that may change or need some adjustment to compensate for new realizations tomorrow.

———————————————————

—

———————————————————

—

———————————————————

—

_____
—

_____
—

_____
—

_____
—

_____
—

_____
—

_____
—

Next, I want you to think about your values—
the standards and principles you live by. Think
about what means the most to you in terms of
how you see yourself involved in this world. **If
you knew you couldn't fail, what would you
be and do?** I want you to write down your top
five values and think about how each of these
values influences your life.

Most individuals have specific values based on their childhood; however, values can change. In order for you to understand more about yourself, I am going to ask that you **write down five values that coincide with you and everyday living.** *What things do you value the most? Do you value commitment? Time? What about loyalty? How about integrity? A particular culture?* There are many different values that you need to determine—what things do you hold most valuable? This will help you to identify your true self. Your deepest values are non-negotiable!

As Socrates stated "Know thyself!"

"Why?" you ask. If you are able to define your values, you will understand what makes you tick and keeps you energized and going. In this, you learn to appreciate your beliefs and norms, enabling you to make wiser and consistent decisions based on those beliefs. As you build a foundation upon everything that you personally value and believe in, you will be ready to move on to the next challenge—and follow successful stepping stones. **Please list your top five values— these are your principles or standards of behavior; your judgment of what is important in your life.**

1.

_____

_____

_____

2.

_____

_____

_____

3.

_____

_____

_____

4.

_____

_____

_____

5.

_____

_____

As human beings, innately we are all wired to want to leave behind a significant legacy that will be remembered. It is naturally ingrained in us to have a desire to live a life full of purpose. We desire to leave something special "about us" to our children and our children's children, or our community.

The good news—you are living in an exciting time in history; you can choose to leave the legacy you desire for your life. In so many ways, we are all able to create our desired destiny if we use what is available to us. Information, and even the schooling and training we are seeking are available at our fingertips, due to technology. We are able to connect with practically anyone, anywhere. The possibilities for our future are endless. So, please make your legacy count: research, read, create, write, love, smile, laugh, study, connect, learn and LIVE!!

One thing that always gives me a sense of confidence and reassurance is to write down what I have completed when working toward my dreams, goals and vision. Don't hesitate, initiate!

I would like you to take a few minutes now to reflect on your current life vision. **Please write down at least three things that you have already accomplished.** This book is not just about learning but about celebrating our successes. If you have been able to move to a destination point that is calling your name and taken action steps, please share them here. You will see the headway that you are already making. If not, please write what you are going to start to do to move forward in this process of getting greater clarity and identifying your next steps.

1.)

_____

—

_____

—

_____

—

_____

—

2.)

_____

—

_____

—

_____

—

3.)

_____

—

_____

—

_____

—

_____

—

Please describe how you are going to incorporate what you learned in Chapter Six. In
what way will you consistently try to implement your *vision*, *personal mission* and
values into your life?

_____

—

_____

—

_____

—

_____

—

CHAPTER 7

CREATING YOUR PLAN OF ACTION

Congratulations! You are ready to create your unique, very own action plan. Yes, you are well on your way, so don't slow down now. Instead, let's pick up the pace. Remember, I am running next to you in this race—and giving you tips and tools for you to take on your journey.

We are still only in the beginning stages of what we need to do together; I encourage you to keep up the pace, so that you can begin to apply all of the hard work you've done up to this point. We have been going through strategic steps in order for you to understand more about yourself, because the more you know *about you*, the more you will know what you want out of life. Is your mission and a fresh vision for your future beginning to gel?

Truly, it does not matter the circumstances you are in. No matter how challenging or dire a life situation can seem, what you want to come true is right in front of you. You must simply be willing to actively step forward as you adopt the mindset of thinking about what is possible. Think positive and be encouraged, all the time remembering that you are good enough to achieve your expectations for your life.

The first step of the action plan is quite easy. I want you to write down the direction you feel that you are headed. Pick a word that states the core goal, and then a word associated with the direction that goal will take you. This may sound silly, but it is a great way to stay focused. Here's an example. I am working toward helping *youth* (the word that states my core goal) reach their potential, and I am headed *upward and onward*—to shoot straight for the stars with my action plan, which stated more specifically, is to provide sophisticated workshops to high school and college students, along with further developing my Facebook business page and You Tube channel with videos to inspire individuals to succeed in their personal life and career.

- _____ (Word)

- _
  (Associated Direction)

Visualize your goals! Be as descriptive as you can be with them—and you will begin to see how realistic they will become. Writing them out will get you in the race and keep you on track. Try not to deviate from the direction you feel strongly that you want to go. It is incredibly challenging to be focused all the time, but having a simply stated plan in place (with a clear goal and direction) will help keep you from being distracted—particularly because it is the basis for specific steps you will take to reach your goals faster and easier.

The next step is for you to think about your bright and shiny goal that you have in your mind. If you are drawing a blank and can't seem to come up with any goals at this point, then start brainstorming some of them today, so that you can begin to map out your future.

I would like you to initiate your goal or goals by thinking in terms of months. This can be very challenging, especially if you are at a young age, to think about goals in the long term spectrum. But this suggestion will help. Goals can be thought of in "SMART" terms. SMART goals stand for:

- Specific

- Measurable

- Attainable

- Realistic

- Timely.

I first learned of SMART goals in my master's program and it really helped me see that I was not being specific enough. As I began doing so, this helped me get on track and stay on track. Obviously, the specifics of your goal can be challenging, especially if when you are confused about what exactly you want, so I came up with my own way to become more detailed. I call it CIKA, which stands for: *Clarity Is Key Always*. This is true for anything that you pursue in life. You must have clarity—"the state of being clear." The clearer you are about what you want, or what you are trying to attain, the more people will understand you and what you are striving toward—and the more you will understand yourself and your goals!

Let's start with **_three goals that you would_** **_like to achieve within the next six months._** This can be starting to learn a new language, getting accepted into a school, finishing school, improving your grades, applying for a particular job, writing a book, starting a new career, moving to a new city—anything that you want. It needs to be as specific as possible, though–remember CIKA. *Clarity is Key Always!*

1. _____
_____
_____
_____
_____
_____
_____
_____
_____

2. _____
_____
_____
_____
_____
_____
_____

_____

_____

3. _____

_____

_____

_____

_____

_____

_____

Next, we are going to look at what you are willing to give up in order to achieve these specific goals. This can be tricky, especially if you are used to spending time on habitual activities daily, such as cruising Facebook, watching your favorite television show, and other recreation or hobbies. Consider what you are doing on a daily basis. Are you currently playing video games all the time? Are you sitting around talking on the phone with friends? Are you watching the television for hours on end? Are you spending hours on social media? These are all stagnant distractions, that if you are doing them on a daily basis, you may need to consider replacing them with things that are going to help your growth rather than hinder.

As many gurus on life have said *"If you are not growing you are dying."* Human beings need continual growth in order to truly thrive in life. Productive days and feeling accomplished feels really good, and also confirms that you are heading in the right direction. If you sit like a couch potato all too often, it is going to be very hard for you to feel as though you are completing anything that will head you in the direction of accomplishing even one goal. In the past, I can recall times when I was more idle than others; not because I was choosing to take a sabbatical, rather I was consumed with activities and motivations that were not helping me to be my best self and work towards my goals. I was distracted and it prevented me from moving forward. It is easy for any of us to fall into the trap of getting stuck in a pit for a period of time. It is quite common, but the solution to not becoming distracted is to avoid becoming immersed in activities that are not contributing to your goals. It seems simple, but can be challenging, especially if you are comfortable in your specific activities and lifestyle. If you remember *why* you want to make the changes in your life a reality it will be much easier to make the necessary adjustments.

For our next step, I want you to think about three things that you are willing to give up in order to create the necessary clarity that moves you toward your potential. Seriously, what are you willing to give up? Rid yourself of the negative energy or time sucking activities, and turn your time into positive productivity that benefits you.

How productive you are, goes hand-in-hand with your influences. Remember, your associations make a statement about who you are, and influence what you say and do. For example, if you are surrounding yourself with people that do nothing but watch T.V. all day long, you will most likely be doing the same thing. In this *unleashing your potential* activity, I want you to concentrate on specific things you are doing, along with any other influences that are holding you back from spending time pursuing your life's ambitions. Be candid, and list as many as seem necessary.

_____
_____
_____
_____
_____

_____

_____

_____

_____

_____

_____

_____

_____

_____

_____

_____

_____

_____

_____

_____

_____

_____

_____

_____

_____

_____

_____

Good job! You have written down some things, or maybe even listed some people you are going to give up spending time with. Giving up anything in life is never an easy task. This can be very challenging for you until you master, mind over matter to aim towards the good things you want. If you can separate yourself from negative and nonproductive people, and materialistic conveniences that are just a waste of your time, you will change your life. Remember, it takes 21 days to break or create a habit.

Try doing this: I feel one of the greatest habits to incorporate is reading books or materials that feed your mind with new information and motivation—every day. Even if you are only able to read for ten minutes when you wake up and ten minutes before you go to bed, you will take in an extensive amount of information. If possible set aside twenty minutes a day to read. Do you think you would be able to work that into your schedule? Please try.

Try doing this: The next thing I recommend is for you to recognize what you do in your personal schedule each day of the week. Realistically think about what you typically do on a daily basis. Be as thorough as possible. *Please write down the good, the bad, and the ugly. Anything you think you would typically do, just write it down.* How is your time spent? Estimate the amount of time doing each of the things you list. Seeing these in writing might make you happy or it might shock you!

SUNDAY

_____

_____

_____

_____

_____

_____

_____

_____

_____

_____

_____

MONDAY

_____

_____

_____

_____

_____

_____

_____

_____

_____

_____

_____

TUESDAY

WEDNESDAY

THURSDAY

FRIDAY

SATURDAY

_____

_____

_____

_____

_____

_____

_____

_____

Now, look back on what you wrote each day. Think about the negative things, or the things that are distractions or a complete waste of time that stand in the way of taking action toward your goals. Also think about the positive things you are doing that you should do even more of each day. I look at myself as someone who genuinely cares for your ultimate success, and in order to conquer negativity and distraction, my goal is to help you get rid of the things that are not benefitting you or holding you back. This unfortunately also is true for relationships. If there is an individual you are spending all of your time with and they are not encouraging you forward, or are not in line with your values, or what you believe to be your purpose and passion, then it will be very difficult for you to proceed to live out your potential. Think about it as two oxen pulling a cart; one is pulling one way and the other is pulling the other way, you can see how difficult it is to move together in a forward motion. Does anyone come to mind that is pulling you in an opposite direction?

I have to tell you—I am so proud of you for continuing to read through this book. Just by doing that, you have made the choice to be relentless about moving forward. When you want something bad enough, through strategic planning, taking action and motivation you are sure to get there! As with anything else, this process takes time.

Now, think about positive things that you need to incorporate into your schedule. How much reading are you doing per week? (This counts!) How much research or study are you doing a week on a particular subject? What are you doing for physical activity to keep your body in shape? These are all questions that I would ask any student that I am coaching. Because at this point, you are consciously making a decision to separate yourself from the masses. You are about to move above and beyond to better yourself. You will be able to excel at light speed as you continue to follow your plan—and *again remember to stay on track*.

You, *yes you*, can make a positive difference in this world, by being proactive and taking ownership of your life. Don't settle on being a student, employee or entrepreneur that is average. Pursue great works and have the backbone to walk through difficult times and look for new opportunities. There is hope for something better in your life. Success is a choice, proven by wanting something badly enough that you persevere to make it happen.

There is no easy way to climb to the top of a mountain. And it does not matter how you do it—whether you are running, walking, or climbing to the top, there will always be significant challenges. You will go through pain and struggles to reach that pinnacle. But just imagine how it will feel when you make that first big milestone? Isn't it going to be worth it? And be sure to appreciate your life and the entire journey of experiences along the way.

Bits of wisdom about life:

- Life is not about instant gratification.

- Reliance on instant gratification strips away the chance to build strength and character.

- Appreciation for life's greater good

comes to those who courageously overcome struggles in life.

- Generosity of time and spirit is returned to those who offer it.

- Impatience causes individuals *to settle* for the wrong person—it's wise to wait for the right timing and right person in important relationships.

- Ask any successful person. Each one has had to deal with struggle and strife at one point or another in their lives.

- Never Give Up—despite what others may say or do. If what you were doing was easy then everyone would do it. The road to success is narrow, but extraordinary.

Wait and see! It's exciting to go through some times of struggle, and then after lots of hard work and growth, get a break! When you finally get that opportunity, you realize that those challenges you went through were all worth it. Consider trying one of these... Instead of watching "Dancing with the Stars," watch a fact-filled documentary that could pertain to your personal growth and broaden your knowledge; instead of going out to a bar or party on a Friday night, have fun attending a networking event that could provide you new insight and potentially open up doors for your career. Think about productivity versus distraction—creative and fruitful versus commotion and interruption. These are all your choice, but the longer you sit back and prolong making the productive steps you need to take, the longer until you attain your goal and purpose in life. *Please write down five positive life choices that you would like to incorporate into your schedule on a weekly basis.* After you write them down, to make them a habit read them out loud every day— no excuses!

1. I will

    _____

    _____

    _____

    _____

    _____

    _____

    _____

2. I will

_____
_____
_____
_____
_____
_____
_____

3. I will

_____
_____
_____
_____
_____
_____
_____
_____

4. I will

_____
_____
_____
_____
_____

_____

_____

_____

5. I will

_____

_____

_____

_____

_____

_____

_____

_____

Doesn't it feel good? I love these exercises!
They are so much fun and it leaves such a
great taste in your mouth after you read them
aloud! In accumulating new and positive "I
will's" and beginning to put them into action,
you are proclaiming and making it known, the
intentions of your life. One of my favorite
Bible versus (from Luke 6:45) suggests, *"A
good man, brings good things from the good
stored up in his heart."* The more we share
with the world of our positive intentions, the
more goodness will come to us from it.

Understand that nothing is going to stop

you but yourself. There is no one who can hold you back, but your own lack of discipline. No one can take away your hopes and dreams, because you are in control of your own destiny. I am providing you the steps; you just need to be committed to implement them.

If I were talking to you face-to-face, I would look you straight in the eye and I would tell you that you are here for a purpose and don't you EVER forget that. Make your time here count! I know there are so many young adults and individuals who have fears, distorted views of the way they feel and look, and have a hard time feeling like they are good enough. I don't ever want you to doubt your piece of the universe. You have the ability to be a successful person in whatever field you choose to take on.

In my parent's back yard, rainbows always portrayed good thoughts and feelings; a great reminder that there is always hope—even if it's a rainy day!

The next task you will complete is to write down your influences and associations. This is very important because it can allow you to see, with fresh eyes, what type of people surround you. Remember the old saying; *you are who you associate with*. It tends to be pretty accurate. If your friends all are lazy and have no ambition the chances of you not being motivated are going to be much higher because you are constantly surrounded by them. If your friends are all entrepreneurs, you will be more likely to become an entrepreneur! This really is common sense. Think about the positive activities you *could* involve yourself in. You need to take a serious look at your influences so that you can get rid of the unacceptable and replace them with the good and acceptable!

List the top five most influential people in your life. These naturally are the people that you associate with the most. After you write the individual's name, I want you to write why you are affiliated with that person. What good purpose does he or she serve in your life?

Name

_____

Purpose

_____
_____
_____
_____
_____

Name_____
__

Purpose

_____
_____
_____
_____

_____

Name_____

__

Purpose

_____

_____

_____

_____

_____

Name_____

__

Purpose

_____

_____

_____

_____

_____

Name_____

__

Purpose

_____

_____

_____

_____

_____

This helps you evaluate your relationship with each of these individuals and decipher whether or not they should be a part of your life. Questions to ask yourself about each of these individuals:

- Does he or she influence you positively or negatively? This is a black and white situation and <u>it can only be one or the other</u>.

- Who are you as a person when you are with him or her? <u>Does who you are when you are with him or her line up with your values</u>?

- How does this person <u>make you feel</u> when you are around him or her?

- How does this individual fit into your life? You must decide who should be in your life—where, when, and why.

- What does he or she <u>add positively, or disrupt negatively</u>?

- How do other people feel about him or her?

I want you to know that if you have found that most of your influences are negative, you can look at this new realization positively. At least you now know what you need to do. *You will need to detach yourself from your negative relationships.* If you remain stagnant and continue to surround yourself with negative influences then your life will remain the same, or potentially get worse.

In a number of cases, of those I have seen that decided to do nothing about making necessary changes with regard to negative influences, their lives continued to move in a downward spiral, For some it took completely hitting rock bottom to decide it was time to make a change. And hopefully, if needed, you will make the right adjustments before things get to that extreme point.

It is, however, encouraging to know that there are also many individuals making good decisions about who they associate with, and in return feel the encouragement and support of those around them. It may be hard to eliminate all relationships that are negative, especially when certain individuals are a part of your inner circle, such as family, but you must not allow anyone to influence you in a way that they will hinder your ability to succeed. You can choose to limit the time spent with them, and dedicate the majority of your efforts and energy to spend time with those who lift you up.

Change is Good

Change is good because it evokes courage and life lessons, causing modifications and alterations, and brings new meaning, along with new found opportunities that often arise. It's also good to ask yourself when something unplanned or unwelcome happens to you: "What did I learn from this experience?"

Change is sometimes an option we choose and sometimes it isn't. Change is difficult for those who get so comfortable that they don't want to move in any different direction. Of course, some individuals will adapt easier than others, but we all have the ability to learn how to make changes when necessary.

At this point I want you to look at your current situation, and if it is not exactly where you want to be and you are ready to make a change, speak out and say, loud and clear "I am ready to make a change!" Good job I am so proud of you! When you voice what you want to accomplish it is so much more effective than simply thinking it.

To help you further commit to what needs to change, please write down five things that you know you need to change in your life in order to achieve your ambitions. For example, if you want to finish your college degree in four years, you need to get off your cell phone or quit watching so much television. If you are doing either (or anything else) excessively, please write it down as something that you need to change. *I encourage you not to waste your time or your mind!*

My perspective on television is to watch it as minimally as possible, and instead, engage in reading and writing. I also wanted to bring light to significant effects technology is having on students and people in general. If you have a cell phone I am sure you are familiar with T9 (this only exists on phones with a numerical keyboard, which largely don't exist anymore), which spells the word out for you or maybe you have an automatic word creator that finishes all of your words. Most of us do not realize the negative effect this has on us, but it is something that is becoming more and more problematic in our society. We are not using our brains the way we used to. I found

157

myself a couple of times asking how to spell a word, and I decided that from then on I was going to spell out the words so that I don't get used to a computer doing all of the thinking for me. I want you to challenge yourself to do the same; continue using your brain like you did before there was access to all of these fancy technologies that think for you. That way, you won't always need to take out a calculator or have every word spelled out for you.

We have become overly dependent on our technology to do everything for us and the effects are negatively impacting us. I am encouraging you to be as proactive and independent as possible, so that when the opportunities arise to put on your thinking cap you are able to do so because you are constantly engaging your brain.

Next I want to be able to do a little activity with you that is going to get you thinking outside the box. **What if I told you that you would never fail no matter what you chose to do in life?** I bet you would feel a little different about trying to conquer your fears and attain your goals than you do now. Let's pretend that's the case. **What goals would you pursue at that point—if you could not fail?** I want these goals to be ambitious, but also realistic. Write down three goals so that you can get an idea of what you would be pursuing without fear. Fear is the number one thing that holds most of us back, so by eliminating the fear of failure you rid yourself of all worry—go for it!

1._____

_____

_____

_____

_____

_____

_____

2._____

_____

_____

_____

_____

_____

3._____

_____

_____
_____
_____
_____ Good
job!

See! Wouldn't life be easier if we were able to be completely fearless! There is no reason to live in fear, because fear will do nothing but paralyze you. My mother always told me in any situation the worst case scenario is death. Since that is highly unlikely, you have just made yourself tougher! I discuss taking risks, never giving up, and failure vs. triumph, for this very reason. I want you to look fear straight in the face and be ready to attack and overcome it at any given moment. You are unstoppable and determined—and you have a will to live strong! Going forward, I want you to wake up each day and state that you are ready to take on life's challenges—ready to put the goals that you desire to achieve *into consistent action*.

Fear is gone! I used to be terrified to speak on stage. When you are confident and believe in yourself, you can accomplish anything. Public speaking now is one of my greatest passions.

CHAPTER 8

HOW TO IMPLEMENT
YOUR GOALS

Dreams require action!   One of my favorite students, Lucas, is the perfect example. He has a dream to become a successful photographer and run his own business. He has some college credit hours, but after going through a few classes he realized that his true passion was photography, so going forward, he has chosen to take classes associated with photography, rather than taking the college degree route.

College is not for everyone, even though getting a higher education is a good route to take. However, it is important for students not to waste time and money with education that will not personally benefit them, or pertain to their future career. You may be like many other students who are having a terrible time narrowing down your education major because there are so many different options, or perhaps you have already completed school and are in a transitional period where you are trying to make some major career or life changes.

You may feel lucky to have lots of options in life, since you can do most anything that you ever imagined through education and hard work. Once you have a clear goal about what you want to pursue, you can get your needed education, apprenticeship or workshop training, which is part of your plan of action.

In our competitive world, it is important to receive some form of continuing or advanced education so that you have the knowledge and skills required to attain success in your specific field. Sometimes that simply means gaining additional knowledge through a program that offers a certificate of completion in something specialized. For example, when I decided to become a coach, I went through the Life Purpose Institute. It gave me a myriad of information to become influential and marketable in my field. This has given me more confidence and more information and methods for me to pass on to help others. This additional training has helped differentiate myself from others with the same college degree. It is important to consider the best ways to be competitive in your field. How can you stand out and be seen as different?

I would like to save you time and money if possible. With students, time and again I see all too many who are not happy with the path that they have chosen—they have regrets and wish they had taken a different course of action. I always remind students that I work with that *there are no wrong choices in education*. All learning has value. Courses previously taken can be applied to life, regardless of whether or not they end up being part of their current field.

Statistics tell us that most people change their career five times in their lifetime. If you desire to change your career, just try to make sure you are pursuing something that you love —there is much more to consider than the money. Unless it is absolutely necessary, never take a job or choose a particular career just for the money—you may end up miserable. You can, however, take a job, get experience, earn income, and from there decide where you want to work more permanently.

High school age and college age students,

sometimes ask me what they can do with a psychology degree or a music degree—or something of that nature. I adamantly tell them, "Plenty!"

I encourage them to make a shift of mindset by considering how people can benefit from what they love to do—provided through their unique personality and in their own creative way, versus what others do that seems more mainstream. Bottom line, how can they stand out and be different? And no matter what, being passionate about what you do in life is a bonus in itself! There are far too many individuals who stay in jobs they hate, so no matter what your dreams or passions are, you have the ability to work towards accomplishing them. If you are willing, there are always steps to get there.

First, know this:

- *Nothing worthwhile happens overnight.* Even if you have to stay in a job you don't like for a while, *get moving in the new direction.* Every step brings you that much closer to your goal and dream.

- *Identify whom or what is holding you back.* Is it fear of criticism? Disappointing someone else? Lack of confidence in yourself, or fear of the unknown? Overcome it.

- *Try getting a "job shadow" opportunity, volunteer, or do more research regarding the type of work or job you want.* Ask questions about education needed, experience required, etc. It may be different than you think.

- Now, start putting what you know about the direction you want to go— *into action!*

The college degree or continuing education that you choose will obviously lead you in a specific direction. After you choose a path to follow, whether it be through a degree, internship, employment, or a developing entrepreneurship, next start thinking about *bringing out your inner most desires and determining more precisely what you would like to accomplish on this path.* **Below, write three accomplishments you want to see happen in your career dreams:**

1._____

_____

_____

_____

_____

_____

_____

2._____

_____

_____

_____

_____

_____

_____

3._____

_____

_____

_____

_____

_____

_____

Having a focus is not hocus pocus! Focus can be incredibly challenging and very frustrating to achieve on a daily basis. For this reason *you* **have** to determine your personal WHY—know what truly inspires you—why is it something you must do? *Embrace your passion by putting it into action!* You will think and act with purpose when you are motivated by your WHY. It keeps you focused. It is the foundation for doing what you do, and it helps establish the habits and actions that will position you to be and do your best. In your daily life, and each time you become distracted, bring this into the forefront of your mind. *Your personal WHY gives you the reason to work so hard toward what you want to accomplish.*

My personal WHY is to help young adults fulfill their dreams. I feel there is a strong need for them to receive direction that will lead them into economic satisfaction and stability. Through my entrepreneurship programs for students, I plan to speak to them around the nation—with a message so strong that it will ignite fires in individual hearts and spread around the globe. This passion comes straight from my heart. I have a burning desire to make a difference in the lives of others—especially young adults.

When your WHY is strong enough, then you will then figure out HOW. For many, it is the how that is the most difficult part. To begin is not always easy—and to rid yourself of excuses can be tricky. People can make excuses all day long about why they are not accomplishing anything, but believe this: there is no excuse great enough to stop you from becoming who you desire to be and *need* to be! I say *need* because it is driven by a dire need that rises up from deep within you—it is something that you must do! Your personal WHY for life is a powerful driving force, and it requires discipline and responsibility that supports it. Once you have accepted that you are going to put your personal WHY into action, you are ready to take the steps needed in order to achieve your success—by taking one day at a time. I can't say this often enough: *Unleashing your potential is a process*. It is not an overnight happening. Instead, it is a constant journey of growth that consistently stretches you to courageously reach for new opportunities, make new connections and gain valuable experience.

Below, please write what you feel your personal WHY seems to be at this moment in time. Even if you are not absolutely sure, you probably do know what drives your passions—and motivates specific actions—and that is what gives you the hope of achieving a goal or dream. If you cannot come up with a personal WHY then write your most prominent passion. I know you have one that stands out, and maybe even more than one!

_____

_____

_____

_____

_____

_____

_____

_____

_____

_____

_____

_____

_____

Next, write down your greatest dream! If you could have anything in the world come true in your life, what would it be? Remember, you need to be specific.

Imagine it, and then write down the *what*, *why*, *when where* and *how* you can see yourself achieving your dream:

_____

_____

_____

_____

_____

_____

_____

_____

_____

_____

_____

_____

_____

_____

Do these specifics correspond with the personal dream you've imagined? If nothing else, it should more clearly reflect your dream in words. *Remember, your greatest dream is the strong desire within your heart to achieve something that is personally fulfilling and increases your future potential.*

I want to take a minute to play devil's advocate with these thoughts for your reflection:

- Is your dream all about achieving what you want in life? If it is only about you, you will live an unfulfilled life.

- Is it strictly based on your personal needs and wants? I want to caution you on this, because if you are living solely to attain only your personal ambitions, I encourage you to take a second look. Reassess how your dream can overflow to benefit others.

- Pursuing your dreams, should include

what you want to change, help, influence, give, and appreciate in others—and so much more to make the world a better place.

- Look at how your dream is going to affect others? If you are a musician, what do you want your audience to hear? If you are a manager, how do you want to interact with your employees? If you are a teacher, how do you want

to positively influence your students? Always insert your WHY in whatever you do.

- Unleash your passion *that is <u>inside</u>*—to positively affect and influence others

173

on the <u>outside</u>!

Heading out to LA, outside of Utah. This open road has endless possibilities, just like you!

One of my greatest life goals as a Midwest girl was to move to Los Angeles. Ever since I was in grade school, I had wanted to pursue living and working there. I don't know why I had such a strong desire to go there, other than it seemed to be the land that was alive with opportunity. It was one of those decisions that required a lot of thinking, because at the time my entire life was built around Chicago and I would be leaving everything that I knew.

Sure, I went on family vacations, but I had never lived anywhere outside of the Chicago area. I recall sitting alone on my friend's rooftop and looking out over the skyline and asking myself if the unknown was really what I wanted. The sense of familiarity felt so secure. I had a great job, I was living in a beautiful apartment by myself, and had been given the opportunity to buy my grandparents condo on Michigan Avenue for a price that I could never get elsewhere. Still, I knew what my heart was telling me—and that was to make the move; a decision that would change my life forever, and also the lives of those around me that loved and cared about me. I felt as though this move was something I needed to do for myself; I didn't want to have regrets. What was possible? I had to find out.

When I made the decision to actually move there, I felt a release of adrenaline and excitement that I had never felt before. I was exhilarated about all of the possibilities that awaited me. My heart sang as my mother and I drove out there anticipating the life that I would lead. Everything would be new and I would be officially opening a different chapter in the book of my life.

I share this story because I want to encourage you if you feel this way about something that is important to you, don't wait around for it to manifest itself because it probably won't. You need to make the decision to take responsible action and go for the dream that lights you up. No one can do it for you, just like no one could make the decision for me to go out to California. I can tell you, for me that it was the best life decision I ever made. I changed, and many other good things happened due to the fact that I chose to listen to my heart and make the move.

It all starts with you making a choice. Pursue your dream or not? From there, it's all about how you will take action on them. Implementing your goals is a process that is based on a strategic plan—this plan parallels the actions that are accomplished. Restated: all of your goals are in alignment with what you want your action plan to be today—and become tomorrow. You need to be organized and have everything mapped out in a bigger scope and strategic plan. This defines your direction; you make decisions on how you allocate resources (e.g. Time, skills, money, self-discipline, confidence, etc.) as you pursue your strategic plan.

Don't let "strategic planning" scare you. Strategic planning is none other than deciding to create a plan for your life—a blueprint—and one that guides you to realize your goals, accomplishing one at a time. To be very accurate, I believe it is better defined as strategic *learning*, *thinking* and *doing*, week-by-week and month-by-month, rather than actually planning everything out from here to eternity. Implementing your goals is completely practical and possible, you just need to remain focused and disciplined to continue moving in a forward motion, as you follow your personal plan. Where are you now? The idea is how to get from there, "Point A" to "Point B" and so on, until you get where you are trying to go. Think about your options at this point. How can you begin to implement your goals? Let's look at how to organize your day-to-day agenda.

I suggest that you have a personal calendar that has daily, weekly and monthly options, to provide timeline accountability with what you will be accomplishing. I highly recommend that you have multiple calendars, one big calendar that shows the entire month at a glance, and a weekly calendar that can go on your wall (I use a dry erase), and then a daily calendar book that you take with you wherever you go. Your cell phone can come in handy as well if you are more of the techie type. I have a calendar on my cell phone, but I personally prefer to write down tasks and activities.

4. Obviously your top priorities will be your daily needs and essentials, along with tasks that are necessities to be completed on the given day.

5. Next, you will delegate your weekly needs and tasks. Write them down

so that you are very clear about your expectations for yourself. This helps with time management.

6. Lastly, your daily assignment will be to go through each day, making sure that you accomplished the three things that you have set out to do (as explained in the earlier chapter).

7. Reward yourself in some way to further encourage and recognize working hard.

Always implementing goals is not an easy task. Sometimes it takes reorganizing your day, making personal changes, or having the fortitude to give something up in order for goals to be attained. Focusing on the task at hand is the key. It's a fine balance to be working and looking toward the future, while living in the moments of today, staying focused and completing the tasks at hand to the best of your ability. It's not always fun, but necessary. This goes back to what you learned earlier about distractions in your life, and being able to rid yourself of them in order to be successful. It is very difficult to concentrate, let alone be productive, if you are consistently distracted by other people, television, drama—and the list goes on.

Please describe your biggest take away from Chapter Eight. What are your next action steps going forward?

_____

_____

_____

_____

_____

CHAPTER 9

ENJOYING THE RIDE

Memories! When I was a little girl, my mom would take me out to the back yard in the early morning. The sun would peek over the trees with its warm intense rays. The dew would dangle on the tips of the grass blades and birds of every kind that scattered throughout our acreage seemed to call out to me with their beautiful sounds. I recall a distinct feeling of hope as the sun rays began to break. My mom constantly reminded me that it was a brand new day and that there were endless possibilities to pursue. We would often hang out for a few hours in the backyard and talk about all kinds of things!

I was a very inquisitive child, and was so curious about the way the world worked. One day I noticed the words on her favorite coffee mug that she carried with her. It had a young woman on it and it said, "Admitting you're thirty isn't easy, it takes five or six years." I used to think about the meaning, and finally, I asked her about it. I said, "Mom, what does that mug mean?" She looked at me and laughed and probably couldn't imagine why I was wondering. I was seven at the time and just like most every kid, I wanted to grow up really fast. I never could understand why someone would want to be younger than their age. I always thought that being older and wiser was better. My mom shared with me that I would understand when I am older, and now, of course, I can really appreciate the saying on the little mug that she carried with her each day.

And like most people, I grew to understand that much of the time we don't appreciate the importance of how moments pass us by. *The little daily things in life accumulate to become the big things!* We need to understand that every day and every stage in our lives are special.

My personal perspective on life is that there are three ways to live it. Look forward to a good future; cherish amazing memories of the past—and most importantly, enjoy the moment we are living, which is our here and now. We never know when it will be our final hour, therefore, it is so important to try and appreciate this very moment. It magnifies living each day to the fullest, and that is what makes all the difference in our todays and tomorrows. Like my parents told me, there is an incredible future ahead of you—with endless possibilities.

My dad lifting me to the sky.
We were both "enjoying the moment."

It's interesting as we look back at our childhood and remember how we always wanted to be older and grown up—and then once we are older we want to be younger. We often want what we can't have. Instead of appreciating where we are in life, we wish for something else. My point—do not allow yourself to fall into the rut of a mindset where you are never satisfied with your current stage of life. Appreciate yourself and others in a way that brings you freedom from trying to be in a place other than the present. Even if you are going through difficult times, remember that you are building a base of personal strength that will be useful for everything you do in the future. And if you are someone who is constantly dwelling on the past you will create a very pessimistic viewpoint of life and therefore, not experience it in the best possible way. Your potential will skyrocket when you simultaneously value the present moment and optimistically look toward the future.

I laugh thinking about how my dad always told me that I said more words in a day than he said in his entire life. He is not one to have an extensive conversation; however, when he speaks, he always leaves a strong impression. He used to tell me that life is *immense!* What a statement, and one that I have never forgotten. It made me appreciate the importance of all aspects of life as incredible, even the challenging ones. They are not to be taken for granted—rather to be recognized as diverse, complicated, amazing and powerful. We make our life what it is and we live our days as we choose. We create opportunities and aspire to achieve. Make your life count by appreciating it each and every day.

Whenever possible, when I wake up in the morning, I like to sit on my porch and look out at the beautiful trees that our house backs up to. I sit, wait and listen. I sip my warm coffee or tea and prepare myself for the busy day ahead. It feels good to mentally prepare for my day, and it relaxes any concern or stress. I take time to pray and meditate on my personal blessings, and then feel thankful for the time I have had to experience the vastness of this incredible world.

Taking this time in the morning to be by myself before my kids wake really has allowed me to greatly appreciate each day. Spending quiet alone time gives you the freedom and independence to think, and completely take in the present and passing moments. I encourage you to experience quiet at some point in the day to do this. It helps you to unplug from the busyness of the world around you and find gratitude in your life, whatever its current state.

Find Hope in the Moment

Some children are forced to grow up quickly. Maybe even you have been forced to grow up too fast! Many of the children I worked with in the Chicago Public School system acted older than their age when they were young teens. I was devastated to see these children feeling as though they needed to be adult-like to be accepted. It was all they knew. Most had no one taking care of them at home, little parental supervision, and not a soul who cared. Some of these children had faced challenges I had never even considered. I wanted to affect these children's lives in a positive way. What would it take, and what could I do, to help them learn, and be more happy and fulfilled? I found that engaging the students in a way that made them appreciate the immediate moment, whether it was with art, writing, reading, and goal setting, etc., they learned to value what they were accomplishing in "real time," right now, which in turn helped them value themselves and become more excited about life in general.

Working with these students made me realize a lot of things in myself—especially that I took life for granted. For example, I counted down the hours until I would get off work; I couldn't wait to step into the next project and forget about the last. I was constantly looking to attain the end result and not appreciating the current moment and the journey. I was too consumed with the goals that were ahead, rather than the special moments of right now. I had been letting special moments pass by, without even realizing it.

I'm well aware that it has always been very difficult for me to relax and "enjoy the ride" along the way. But I was forced to change my perspective (not always easy) as I learned how to live in the present moment. I now know that some of the greatest times in life are encountered in the processing of it, and that both you and I will always be a work in progress. Since we are on our life journey for our *entire* life, it is wise to be thankful for all aspects of it. Your story is created from all of your experiences, not just some. It's important to remember the hardships you have walked through, while always remembering the accomplishments, too!

Every day you (and me) are working toward a destination point, regardless of whether you know where that is. You are always working towards something. Now, think about some of the goals that we have created together so far. Instead of thinking about the end result of the goals think about pausing points. Times that you change direction due to failure, or a time when you weren't disciplined to accomplish all that needed to be done. For each stopping or pausing point that you create I want you to pat yourself on the back and reward yourself in some way shape or form. Recognize that a brief diversion from the primary goal is not the end, but only a pause. Look back, and reward yourself for progress you have made along the way, even if your goal is still in process, and not a completed in its entirety. Start again, keep going, and don't give up. There is something more waiting ahead in your life, and you can look forward to that "something!" It is not just a matter of reaching an end result; it is about all those little steps you've taken to move toward your goal, your dream—the starts and stops, the pauses, detours— that you have taken that will eventually get you to your desired destination point.

I can give you an example of exactly what I am looking for and I would like you to create this same exact format through a spreadsheet or word doc. This will enable you to assess your progress.

Goal: I am going to start working on a business plan for my new photography company.

Pausing Point: I have created a website and have developed social media outlets to create exposure for my business.

Reward: I will go to a fancy restaurant to celebrate with a friend.

Everyone needs to feel rewarded; it's important to take the time to show yourself some appreciation. Make sure to do this on a consistent basis because this creates a significant impact on your confidence and energy level—and impacts your ability to look forward as you take action toward significant outcomes.

I am sure that there are a lot of things that you would like to feel rewarded for, and when you do so, you instill yourself with the encouragement needed to continue taking action to reach your goals. You will make things happen one day at a time. Subconsciously this creates a mental habit to work toward a positive direction, because you want to receive the reward for all your hard work. The title of this chapter, "Enjoy the Ride," prompts you to consider each passing moment that you will not get back. Life goes by so quickly—in the twinkling of an eye it is over. Many individuals have a difficult time enjoying the ride and appreciating life today, for whatever it holds. Don't let that be you! Enjoy – benefit from – take pleasure in this very moment!

Obstacles and Trials

There are many obstacles and all kinds of trials and suffering that make up every person's life, but if a person chooses to use them for good, those same struggles will mold and grow us into becoming the person we are meant to be—to maximize potential.

I know that you may be one, like many others, who have been through unbelievably difficult circumstances, and I won't pretend to imagine the effect that it has had on you. But no matter what you have endured, I believe that there are always people or things to be thankful for. I want you to remember that no matter where you are headed, or how far you have to go, there is always a light at the end of the tunnel. Don't ever forget it. **Please write below at least three things that you are thankful for in your life today, and then say them aloud!**

_____

_____

———

Today, you may be in the middle of an experience or challenging season in your life that you don't understand. One that has left you confused or distraught beyond belief. Or it may be the opposite, and today you feel exhilarated like never before. On any given day, you can't control everything that happens to you, but in your intricate life, you can continue to take positive risks to stretch and grow. Keep your head up—knowing that one day you will see the reason for your hardships. They make your reasons for being thankful all the sweeter.

Your life chapters, like everyone's, bring opportunities and sometimes failures, but the important lesson to learn is that no matter how tough life becomes there is fresh hope when the sun rises again tomorrow. True appreciation of life is being able to accept your good times along with the bad. Please know that no matter what, you are going to be okay, because every moment matters to build a completely authentic story of your life!

Please describe how you will try to live more fully in the moment, and/or your big-

gest take away from Chapter Nine. What are your next action steps going forward?

_____

_____

_____

_____

_____

_____

_____

_____

_____

_____

_____

_____

_____

_____

_____

_____

_____

_____

_____

_____

_____

_____

_____

_____

_____

_____

_____

_____

CHAPTER 10

TAKING SMART RISKS

Risk-taking is accepting the fact that there is a positive opportunity that could develop, while at the same time accepting there could be a loss. As we all know, a risk isn't a sure thing; it might be a gamble. However, I am the type of person who likes to walk on the wild side of life—at least a little bit! I walk out there on the edge, and I am what you would call a risk-taker—one who is willing to venture out to accomplish something new and interesting.

Why? Probably because as a child it was ingrained in me to have no fear. My brothers and I were raised to be adventurous free spir-its. We romped around in the woods when it was storming, rode the quad runner in the middle of the night, and climbed to the very tops of the pine trees. We were pretty fear-less, to say the least, and I was always the ringleader.

I still remember the day when my dad took my training wheels off and decided that I should go down the *big* hill on two wheels. Without hesitation, I followed him to the top of the hill with my little purple and white bike, and I was ready to show off. We made it to the top and my dad said, "Okay, now just focus and don't swerve."

I said, "No problem," as I remember thinking to myself, "This will be a piece of cake." My dad said, "Okay, you go first!" I took a deep breath, looked down the hill and went for it! I pedaled so fast my feet came off and I couldn't manage to get them back on the pedals to apply the brakes. I squeezed my legs together hoping that I could control the bike that way and it actually made my steer-ing worse. Before I knew it, the handlebars were swinging back and forth and I completely lost control of my bike. I couldn't slow down and that was when I realized there was no way to try to balance and hold on to stay up-right. I toppled over, face first and landed smack dab on my chin. As you can imagine, I scraped it up big time; I screamed in pain which was only made worse by seeing the blood that oozed out. My dad, being the tough guy that he was, simply said, "Come on Genesis, you're okay. Let's go back to the top!"

This time I wasn't so tough or eager to head back up. I thought to myself. . . *There is no way I am going back up there*. He said, "Come on, let's go. You can do this!"

I managed to stand up, with tears running down my cheeks, and peddled my way back up to the top with my dad leading the way. My chin was pretty bloody, and I remember him taking his white shirt and gently wiping the blood off, while tons of mosquitoes came swarming around me. He confidently said, "This time you're going to do it; don't be scared!"

I knew what I had to do but I was so desperately scared at this point. If I fell again, I would have no chin left so I knew it was necessary to succeed. I prayed for a miracle! I felt a little push from my dad and off I went down the hill. The bike began to pick up the pace and I knew that this was it. I just needed to stay focused and hold on tight. Keeping my feet on the pedals this time, I have never been so in the zone! The closer I got to the bottom the more confident I felt. It was then that I realized I am going to make it! Within moments I zoomed across the finishing point. Whew! I made it. I remember thinking to myself with my bloody chin to prove it; *I am a pretty tough despite getting a little beat up!* I have to thank my dad, because even in the face of fear, he knew that this experience would make me realize that I could always conquer a goal, even if it takes more than once to make it happen. You can do the same!

Sometimes we think to ourselves that certain goals are impossible, especially if we don't have people around us to encourage us to take the risk. When you believe something is impossible you will prove that you are right. Of course, there is so much more to goals than we think, and they are always a challenge—they are difficult instead of easy; that's just reality. For that reason, I stress over and over, "Have the right mindset. Think *you can!*"

Right now, please write down <u>three risks</u> that you are willing to take in order to attain your goals.

EXAMPLES: I will save more money and only buy things I really need. I will not be shy, and network with groups that can increase my opportunities.

1. _____
   _____
   _____
   _____
   _____
   _____

2. _____
   _____
   _____
   _____
   _____
   _____

3. _____
   _____
   _____
   _____
   _____
   _____

What about these risks are especially challenging for you?

_____
_____
_____

_____

_____

_____

Why must you take these risks? What is the payoff for you to you personally or professionally?

_____

_____

_____

_____

_____

Risks are dealt with on a day-to-day basis. You take a risk every time a word comes out of your mouth. You take a risk when you walk down the street, when you fly, or when you stand outside in a thunderstorm. Risks are good because they allow you to overcome fears and live life more fully. **I am not insinuating to take a risk like walking down a dark alley late at night by yourself; I am referring to SMART risks.** "Risk" is important to discuss because there are so many people sitting around in their comfort zone who will never take the risk to test their potential. It is so disheartening to me, when I know certain individuals have the ability to do great works in this world, yet they do nothing towards making that happen. Their potential is dormant and wasted.   I had an interesting experience and an important lesson about the benefits of taking a risk when I became involved with children that lived in the low income housing of Cabrini Green. This was when I attended the Moody Church in Chicago, and I wanted to volunteer my time, so when I came across the opportunity to work for "By the Hand for Kids" that tutored children in Cabrini Green, I jumped on it. Despite the risks that came along with it, I was excited for this opportunity because I felt that it was a great way to give back to children who were desperately in need of adult time, teaching, and encouragement.

If you are not familiar with Cabrini Green, it is one of the most impoverished and run down housing projects in Chicago land. Our job as volunteers was to go into Cabrini and tutor the kids for as long as we could work with them. Many of these children did not have positive role models at home, and they were looking for someone to come into their life and give them a reason to have hope. I felt I had much to offer these children; encouragement and love were imperative in making a difference.

My first day at Cabrini, I made sure that I was dressed in drab, understated clothes. I did not want to stand out in any way and wanted to do all that I could, to hopefully fit in. Hmmm. . . My heart was racing as I pulled up next to the worn down curb in my white Camry and looked out the window. There were many homeless people standing around. By the way they dressed and acted, I could see at a glance that they were involved in drug use and gangs.

To say the least it was very intimidating, and yet I knew my calling required that I have the courage to at least step out of my car. It was a risk I had to take, because I sincerely wanted to offer what I could to make a difference in the lives of these kids who had so little, and few role models to give them direction. So, I did get out of the car, and swiftly walked with purpose up to the door. I tried to open it, but it was locked. For a moment my heart dropped, because I wasn't sure if I would just have to turn right back around and head straight back to my car. I rang the little door bell and almost instantly a woman named Erin answered the door. She was so excited to have me there and welcomed me as a participant in helping these children. My breathing relaxed a little. I was pretty nervous considering I had no idea what to expect from these kids. I thought "What if they hate me?" which made me feel my hands would be tied before I even got a chance. Erin asked me to fill out some paperwork, and then took my picture to prepare a badge for me. After that, she asked the grades I would like to teach and I said, "I can work with any of them."

She said, "Well, you have to start with a few specific grades and then we can go from there." I decided that I would try to work with the younger ones to start. I thought I would like to tutor the first, second and third grades, which was quite exciting for me at the time. I asked when I would be able to get started. Erin said they needed to process my application, which would be done within twenty-four hours, so I planned to come back the next day.

After I left, I felt good about having the courage to step out of my white Camry and my comfort zone. I thought of all of the lives that were going to be changed through this organization, and how it would be an honor to be a part of helping children who needed so much. The next day, after a full day of teaching at my job, I went back and finished my screening process. I was led up the stairs to a long hall that contained about six classrooms. Each room was full of kids. I was very nervous, because I had no idea what these kids were going to think of me, or what surprises might be in store.

Erin said to me, "So you have decided to work with the younger kids, right?" I answered "Yes." She asked me to follow her. She brought me into this bright colored room with all kinds of games, books, and toys. It was like a child's fairy tale. As I stepped closer to the center of the room all of the kids stared at me, and probably wondering. . . *Who is this white lady coming in to disturb their playtime?* All of a sudden, this confident black woman came into the room and said "Everybody take a seat, there is someone you need to meet! Ms. Genesis please introduce yourself!"

I am sure you can well imagine how intimidated I felt, especially as I received the "death look" from so many little kids all at once. I knew, however, that I was there to help these kids and that they were just going to have to accept me, regardless if they wanted to or not. I introduced myself and said hello to each of them making sure that I was as personal as possible. I could see that none of them were very accepting of me. They couldn't trust me yet, and I could see this was going to take some time for them to even begin to accept me. I stayed for a bit, and then called it a day, headed home.

I went back there frequently, and the more time I spent with them, the more they began to accept me into their world. Day-by-day, the kids became more and more attached, and pretty soon they jumped up and hugged me when I walked in the room. It was an amazing experience working with these kids. Working with them, I could feel the sadness and yearning for love that they had.

Some of my little friends I met while tutoring at Cabrini Green in the Chicago housing project.

I felt like a surrogate mother, wanting to let them feel the joy and innocence of being children for the hours I was able to work with them. The more time I spent with them, the more I loved and personally cared about each of these children. Like all of us, all they wanted was love, hope and someone to offer encouragement and say, "You can do this!" just like my dad had told me so many times. The reason for my story is for you to consider the hurt, sadness and discouragement that is in our world today, and there are countless places to affiliate yourself with to make a difference. Look around you, and think of all positive organizations that are making a difference in people's lives. The point is, not only for you to realize how many people need help, but how you can make a difference in someone else's life by taking a little bit of a risk, and offering your help.

Rewards of taking a risk:

- Helps you overcome the fear of trying.

- Creates new possibilities for you to use your skills and gifts.

- Gives a big boost to your self-confidence.

- Provides great lessons and broadens your life experience.

- Brings unexpected blessings and personal rewards.

Yes, I took a risk when I volunteered to work with the kids and go into Cabrini Green. What would those kids think of me? Would they accept my help and attention? I had no clue. I took the risk, because it was worth it to me to follow my mission in life. *To help youth understand they have a good future and huge potential!*

Think about your life mission. *What you would be willing to risk in order to make your dream a reality?* Write "your risk" that you will take in the lines below. Always remember risks are good when they are taken within reason and are physically safe.

Risks mean different things to different people. For some individual's, risk may mean going up to a complete stranger and asking them to take a survey, for others it may be jumping out of a plane to go skydiving, or perhaps you are like many people that just needs to say yes to something that has been nudging at you to pursue for a long time. You can only determine what risks you would be willing to perform under your own personal standards—this is your personal risk. (Example of mine: The children may not accept or like me—that was a big risk that made me feel insecure, and took me way out of my comfort zone. I learned that taking the risk was good, because though intimidated, I managed to change many lives, including my own through the amazing experiences with these children. We tend to think we are going to change other's lives by our actions and much of the time we do, but interestingly enough when we go out to help others grow, we often end up becoming more fulfilled and grow more than we could have ever imagined—because we took that chance to influence someone else's life. That is one of the most beautiful parts about life. Once you have experienced something such as I did at Cabrini Green, you will never again be the same.

Please describe your biggest take away from Chapter Ten and what are the action steps you will consider taking going forward?

_____
_____
_____
_____

CHAPTER 11

TOOLS THAT YOU DIDN'T LEARN IN SCHOOL

School curriculums don't supply some of the most important aspects of living in the real world. It seems the majority of graduates find themselves lost and confused after gradua-tion—and left wondering where the next stage of adult life will take them. If this is you, it is important to know you aren't the only one who has some life learning to do—like effective communication, how to handle money, manners, time management, and the list will go on.

Nor do most schools teach students skills involving networking, relationship building, or marketing and sales techniques. Each of these entities is critical to learn in order for you to be a successful individual. Take a minute and think about anyone who has been able to help you out with things such as getting a job, direction setting, opening a career door, making a helpful connection, etc. These circumstances manifested because you had an affiliation/connection/relationship with another individual. Who you meet is always something to be thinking about when you are looking for new opportunities. Seek out individuals who have knowledge and expertise, and are in positions of power and authority. By seeking out these types of individuals, you are getting access to decision makers. Why not make the effort to get in touch with individuals who make the decisions? Why not start from the top if you can? For example, if you need solid information about an organization or are applying for a job, always ask for the person in charge or who makes the decisions, instead of wasting time or getting the run-around from those who have no influence. There will be many times when there is a gatekeeper who holds the key to getting in front of the right person. Work to be impressive to this individual, talk with them, get to know them—sell yourself. This works in any profession, and most often this will take you a lot further. You can build relationships with anyone given the right opportunity, and the desire and perseverance to do so. Be genuine, respectful, and kind as you build special mentoring or business connections.

Communication is the key to success in anything that you choose to do. Whether you are working on building relationships, meeting new people, interviewing, or anything involving interaction with another human being, you need to have effective communication skills. If you can become a master at these things you will not only be able to run your own business, but you will also be able to become a leader in whatever field you decide to pursue.

- Listen; have empathy

- Exhibit good nonverbal skills – positive body language

- Speak clearly and concisely

- Blend being friendly and confident

- Be open-minded and respectful

- Show interest, respond with feedback

All of those apply as you network, so let's look at the definition of the word "networking." According to www.dictionary.com: Networking is to *cultivate people who can be helpful to one professionally, especially in finding employment or moving to a higher position.*

As you read this definition you can see why it is so important to network with others. Networking is none other than reaching your hand out to people, speaking about each other's individual purpose, interests, business ventures, etc. This type of interaction does not have to be on a grand scale. Networking can be as simple as walking into a retail store and introducing yourself, getting to know the manager and continuing to follow up on building the relationship with sincere interest and communication. This is how relationships are created. If you want that job at the retail store, you can get it! This is perpetuated through the mindset that we discussed before. *Positive mindset equals optimistic results.* Whenever you are networking, be open to learning about others and never forget to authentically listen. Inquiring about and listening to others is one of the most important things that you will ever do because it allows you to understand another person's perspective on specific things.

Whenever I meet someone new, I always encourage them to talk first. This helps them to know they are important to me. When it is my turn, I reciprocate by sharing my information with them. Whatever you do, please don't walk up to someone that you are trying to build a new relationship with and over talk about yourself. Most of the time, he/she will become irritated quite quickly and not take you seriously if you pursue conversation with a "me first" attitude. *Whoever* you are trying to get to know, it is important for you to recognize that he/she is just another person, exactly like you! You have the ability to relate to them regardless of their age or gender or business position. Look forward to attaining more knowledge and gaining more experience from each and every person you meet. Watch how cool it works out to be a win-win!

"Aha" Moments

We are all on our own little life adventure,

and we have these "aha" moments that occur all of the time. An "aha" moment is when you realize something that you may have heard before, but it never really resonated with your heart the way it is right now—this very moment. An "aha" moment can also be something you have never heard or experienced before and then all of a sudden the light bulb in your head goes off. You think to yourself. . . *Okay, now I get it!*

I think there are a lot of things that we learn, but we do not fully interpret or apply them, at least not until something hits us personally or at the perfect moment in time. In an instant, we have sudden insight or new revelation that is profound.

These "aha" moments happen when you stay open-minded, and continue to meet new people with fresh ideas and different perspectives. I encourage you to welcome other's thoughts and become aware of how they might impact you. Expect to have "aha" moments when you meet people and connect with them. One such moment can change your life course, and plunge you into an unexpected adventure or career course. And it is incredible to interact with individuals who have similar life ambitions. It is a beautiful partnership as you parallel the life experiences of

213

others. This happens when you remain open and flexible.

I'm grateful for one of those moments in my own life that happened to me when I moved to Los Angeles. My good friend from Chicago was visiting LA, and invited me to a networking event, saying that I definitely should come—it was going to be great! Even though I had just worked a really long day and was incredibly tired, I thought that it was in my best interest to go. I dashed home to change, hurried back to the car and ran inside to the event, because I did not want to miss any of it. As I entered, I was so excited when I realized that Les Brown (motivational speaker, author, and radio and television host), one of my favorite idols was there. I had seen and heard him through various media; I felt that we shared similar passions for helping young adults to grow, develop, and find hope in life. To meet him in person was a dream come true. I was nervous at first, and wasn't sure how to approach him. I walked into the auditorium and I saw Les standing there. He was surrounded by tons of people wanting pictures and of course to exchange a few words with him. Then, all of the sudden, I had my opportunity to seize the moment and speak to him.

Having no idea what I was going to say, I looked at him and burst out, "I just love you!" He was a little taken back and started laughing.

The truth for me is that he is an amazing

man
and I
just

couldn't hold back my excitement to meet him; his good intentions, and his work that helped young adults overwhelmed and impressed me. We spoke for a few moments and he asked me what I did in life. I told him my vision was to help young adults across the nation to fulfill their purpose, find direction, and achieve their dreams. He was so impressed that he gave me his personal number. To this day, Les and I are friends—and I hope in the near future, we are able to collaborate on creating a fantastic program for youth.

My good friend, Les Brown

I think this story is significant because it shows you how making one decision can have such an impact on your life. I met so many people at that particular event who really impressed me, and if I mentioned each one and how special they were to me I would never finish this book. The list goes on of those that inspire and make a difference in this world. Whenever you have an opportunity to be a part of something where people you admire or consider great gather, you should take full advantage and do whatever it takes to get there. Opening up opportunities for yourself increases the chances that you will run into someone who can put you into the right place at the right time—and perhaps give you an "aha moment."

Success requires you to:

- Get *out there!*

- Gain confidence.

- Gather and mingle.

- Get opportunities by being open to

them.

- Glimpse possibilities.

- Grasp new ideas.

- Be grateful.

Life is full of surprises! You may meet someone who may contact you much later, and has a desperate need of your skills or expertise. YOU NEVER KNOW! Stay aware of all circumstances and people around you, and be approachable and willing to be a part of the opportunities that are presented.

Things that are hard for some of us:

- Reach out and ask for advice from people of all ages!

- Ask questions, even though you may fear looking silly or sounding stupid. (More often than not, someone else has the same question.)

- Look for and ask for a mentor; they are right in front of you. (Teachers, coaches, neighbors, friends, coworkers, bosses, online topic forums, etc.)

The road to unleashing your potential is winding and wide—maybe even endless as you continue to develop tools that you didn't learn in school. As you walk on, I suggest you interact with a mentor as much as you possibly can. Extend your hand, reach out to others, and ask them questions. This can be the beginning of attaining the assistance you need; just ask!

Consider "aha" moments you have experienced. Who was the person that helped make it possible? How are you different today because of this "aha moment?"

_____

_____

_____

_____

_____

_____

_____

_____

I end this chapter by asking you to consider those people who have personally inspired and motivated you.

Who are five individuals that you want to

meet and interact with?

Don't ever feel it is impossible to build a relationship with the great people in your career niche. Meeting Les Brown showed me that anything is possible if we just put ourselves out there enough to make it happen.

As Michael Jordan said, *"You miss 100 percent of the shots you don't take!"*

1.

2.

3.

4.

5.

CHAPTER 12

FAILURE VS. TRIUMPH

There is nothing quite like writing a book if you want to look at where you've been and dream about where you want to go! I realized a lot of things as I went through the process of writing this book and I came to the conclusion that all obstacles that have crossed my path (and yours) are meant to be there for a specific reason. I have grown stronger because I have overcome weakness. And I do know what it feels like to have courage, because I know what it feels like to feel afraid. I'm moving onward and upward in my personal and professional life, learning lessons and gaining wisdom, because I have walked through times of being foolish or feeling foolish. This is me and this is you, because these experiences are all common to the human condition.

Inevitably, we all face challenges—we do things right, we do things wrong, and I dare you to defy the odds and overcome—whatever it is you face! And as you do, your new found strength and understanding of how the world works will feed right into the grand purpose for your existence on this earth. Every tool within this book that I have provided for you is to help you follow that purpose—one which includes your goals and dreams, your vision and mission—and your passion!

It is heartbreaking for me to know young women and men who have so much going for them, and so much to give, but for one reason or another, they are not able to get their lives together to live out their passion and unleash their potential. Some might say it's all about being organized, effective planning, time management, research, education, and choosing to contribute to society by giving back, etc. These are all excellent, but they are only the branches that stem from the primary trunk.

What is your trunk? *Your trunk is your mindset*. It is your very being—the rock of hope and faith, courage and confidence that stirs within you. It is your ability to be able to see past your present circumstance—no matter how unfair or hard it has been, or currently is. It is your determined capability to be able to fully believe in your vision for something greater, something slightly out of reach, and pursue opportunities with tenacity. Think about the big picture here. If you do not have a sturdy trunk that you nourish and allow to flourish, how do you expect your branches to grow?

Please, don't ever underestimate the power of your potential. You have the ability to change not only your life, but the lives of so many others with the skills and gifts you have been given. Your passion can light up the world. Please write below, *"I am a gifted human being with an incredible amount of potential and nothing can come between me and my dreams!"* This is you!

_____

_____

_____

_____

By now you know I want to not only run in the race, but win the race! Of course themes of failure and triumph bring lots of stories to mind; this is one of my dearest memories. In 2009, I decided to run my first marathon. I had never thought that it would be possible to run a marathon considering I am not a long distance runner. In my younger years I participated in the 100, 200, 400 and long jump, so I am sure you can imagine in the mind of a sprinter, going from a 100 meter dash to running in a 26.2 mile run takes *a whole different mindset*.

I actually thought that running a marathon would be truly impossible, but then I thought about all the people who have completed marathons before me. I found myself pondering. . . *There is no reason that I shouldn't be able to complete one successfully. . . if they* (many others just like me) *did it, I should be able to do it, right? So why not just try?*

The morning of the marathon was cool and crisp, only thirty-five degrees in Chicago land. I woke up at 4:00 a.m., extremely excited and nervous about the big day. I quickly got dressed and met my running buddy, Leah, at her house. We took the Red Line down to Grant Park where there were thousands of people gathered together to cheer on all the participants. I had never seen anything like it. Relieved that we were able to get registered quickly, we headed toward the starting line where a distinct nostalgia was in the air; freedom, hope and ambition stirred all around. Each person had their own story; they represented something that they believed in or supported. It was incredible to be a part of this marathon, because it felt as though we all had a strong, individual purpose for taking on this challenge. We each were a puzzle piece to the greater, complete picture. Like in the world as a whole, I feel that we all are a part of a greater purpose working together through our own gifts to make a difference in the lives of others. The time grew closer and I continued to observe the excitement around me. My eyes eagerly scanned over the people throughout the massive crowd, and then all of a sudden I heard a shot ring out and we were off. The longest that I had run up until that point was twenty miles which was two weeks prior so there was still a sense of anxiety for me to finish 26.2 miles.

As my feet began to move, I realized that there is always a first time for everything, and sometimes we have to jump out and take a leap of faith and trust that we can do it—that everything will work out. As thoughts raced through my mind, I looked up and realized the big crowd of runners had all gotten a good start on their journey. Before long, everyone began to throw off their top layers of cloth-ing, so I decided to do the same. I started out at a 10 minute 45 second pace which turned out to be great, because I felt incredibly comfortable and strong. Then gradually, I picked it up, little by little. My goal was to run the marathon in four hours and thirty minutes, which I felt was definitely attainable for my first. There were pacers throughout the race; they carried huge signs. I couldn't get over the fact that they were able to run 26.2 miles and hold a sign that large to encourage the rest of us along the way. It was incredibly impressive!   After I passed the five mile mark I was going strong and running at about a 9 minute 45 second mile, beginning to pick it up. I felt really great and thought. . . *This is going to be no problem, just stick with this pace and I am golden.*

On mile six of the marathon

All of a sudden my right I.T. band started cramping (Iliotibial band, the ligament that runs down the outside of the thigh from the hip to the shin). I thought. . . *Oh no, this can't happen now, not after all of the training I have been through, this is not happening!* I started to panic! I thought "How am I going to run 21 more miles?" But I had already made a firm decision before I started the race. There was no giving up for me at this point or any time later; I would crawl to the finish line if I had to.

Sometimes in life we get so involved in the

pain of certain situations that we don't look at the overall goal of what it is we are trying to accomplish. This was one race I was not going to stop; I was in it to the end. Luckily, there was a drink station every two miles, so on mile six I grabbed a Gatorade and started chugging. While we traveled through the different parts of the city I felt like a tourist going for a long ride, and able to see the sights of every unique location. My life began to flash before my eyes at this point, and I started to reflect back on the all the years of my childhood. I started to think about how each year of my life signified a mile in the marathon and how ironic that I was actually 26.2 years old when I ran the race. It was a very eye opening experience. An "aha" moment in fact, because I realized how everything fit together to make up my story—which included all of the things that I had done up until that point—the good, the not so good, and the dreams I hoped to pursue in my future. It was a beautiful and comforting moment in time.

Near mile fifteen it got very cold and the wind was blowing ferociously. I could feel the air coming through my gloves and my hat. All I could think about is that I was more than half way there. I felt like the   Energizer Bunny that keeps going and going and going. I saw many people walking or slowing down and I thought to myself. . . *I have got to finish*. It does not matter what all of these other people are doing, and I couldn't let it distract me. I was running the race for myself and there was no way that I would change direction or stop my momentum because others were. So true, in every life situation!

I was coming up upon China town, and there were tons of people hollering all over the place, and that was when I heard a woman yell, "Keep going you're almost there!" I looked over at the big sign and I saw MILE 20 and I thought. . . *Wow, only six more miles!* My friend, Leah, was running next to me and doing tremendously well. She said, "Congratulations Genesis, you just passed the 20 mile marker, farther than you have ever run before!" She was right; it was my first time running farther than 20 miles. A strange feeling came over me with each step that I took. I was going out into the abyss, taking steps never before taken and I was just trusting that I could do it! It seemed as though everything was in slow motion and my goal of completing a full marathon was getting closer and closer to a reality. I finally reached mile

25 and I only had one mile left to go! Could it possibly be? At this point my legs were aching with pain, but yet I felt stronger than ever before! I started to round the final corner and with incredible power and ambition ran down the last 200 meters conquering the depths of all my doubts. I saw thousands of people cheering us all on to finish strong. I sped through the line and finished! Words cannot express all of the emotions that went through me as I walked to try and stabilize my legs after fulfilling my dream. I had done it. Wow! For a few seconds I couldn't believe it. I stood there and looked around; tears came down my cheeks and I said aloud, "I did it!" It was one of my most profound accomplishments that I have achieved up to this point in my life.

I highly recommend running a marathon to help you conquer fear, doubts, or frustrations. It will truly change your life, forever. I shared this story with you because I wanted to provide you a visual of your life. No matter where you are at this point in time, you are there for a reason. You are there to inspire others, change someone's life, encourage another and genuinely make a difference. I want you to know that if you live life like a marathon, you choose your destiny. You always have the option to quit, but for you to truly attain your potential and pursue your passion, you can never stop. This may come across as difficult, challenging, frustrating, tiring or unattainable but you can rise above it. With one foot in front of the other, your desire turns into action; it lives and breathes to take you across that finish line.

I encourage you to concentrate everyday on all of the positive facets of your life, as you remember my emphasis on your mindset being the foundation that strengthens all else. Are you questioning whether you have positive aspects about yourself? Then we will create them today. I want you to write five positive words that you want others to define you by and I want you to feel these words and experience these words and say them every day. I will give you some samples: *motivated, successful, ambitious, loving, caring, devoted, determined, attractive, etc.* The words you write are how you want to be, so guess what? You will be if you believe it!

I am _____

I am _____

I am _____

I am _____

I am _____

Saying these five "I AM 's" every single day will ingrain in your mind and heart some of the things you already are aware of that you can turn into positive action. The more you believe these things about yourself, the more you will live them out. The words that you write are significant. They will enhance your mindset to keep you feeling and thinking positive about the person that you are and what you are able to do.

It's true that *you become what you think*— and when you write, speak and think these positive things, you are always ingraining a "can do" perspective and a firm belief in yourself. In turn, you will create positive outcomes in your life. When a negative thought starts to enter your mind, and you have any doubt about yourself, dismiss the thought and replace it with a positive one. If you feel down, do something that makes you feel up! Statistics say that throughout the day 80 percent of our thoughts are negative and 20 percent are positive. Try to turn that statistic around by replacing the negative with positive thoughts. And surround yourself with people and things that increase your confidence level. Play a happy song, talk to a good friend, go for a run, but try to never let yourself be down and defeated—rather, triumph!

Don't Worry – Failure Happens to Everyone

I tell my students that there is no reason to worry about failure because it is going to happen to everyone at some point. We all will fail, but we will learn from our experiences, and use them to apply new learning to our lives and the lives of others. What a cool thing to know—your greatest hardships, in time, bring value to your life that can be your greatest gift to pass on to others. It's good to recognize you are not the only one! Share your story and connect with others. People need you in this world. There are so many individuals calling out for someone just like you to come in and make a difference for them. This is real life, right now, so make the choice to take all of the tools that I have provided for you in this book and apply them.

You are worthy of having a life worth living, you are worthy of making your life count, you are worthy of leaving behind a legacy, you are good enough to create change in other people's lives. One person, then two. . . *But start with you!*

I want to close with you writing this down. "I

_____am worthy of a motivated, purpose-driven life. I am fulfilled daily because I love what I do. I can make a difference in the lives of others through. . . What? You write out the rest. . .

How will you live your life? Make it count!

Do you have questions in your mind that are still unanswered? Write them down, and tomorrow go out and discover the answers.

_____
_____
_____
_____
_____
_____
_____
_____
_____
_____
_____
_____
_____
_____
_____
_____
_____
_____

_____

_____

_____

_____

_____

_____

_____

_____

_____

_____

_____

_____

_____

_____

_____

_____

_____

_____

_____

Closing

Thank you for taking the time to read this work of mine—it is filled with my passion for your success. I am here to help you grow, aid in your development, and instill hope in your life!

I feel that I am none other than a messenger to push you to achieve the most important thing in life—to live your purpose. It is a privilege to serve you and be a part of your journey. I look forward, right along with you, to the exciting ventures you will pursue after you conclude this book. I hope that it helps to keep you in the race, and guides you through life's challenging obstacles. It is my greatest dream that you would reach inside the depths of your soul and find the epitome of what makes you uniquely who you are. I believe in you, and I encourage you to never give up no matter how hard any season of life may seem. And please never forget, you were put on this earth for a good reason. I will never give up on you, so I want you to make me a promise that you will never give up on yourself!

"We are all winners and we all have a journey in life in which we can excel, so follow your heart, and you can never go wrong!"

The WHY of this book. . .

This book was created so that you may personally shorten the learning curve and go after every goal that you see fit for your future. Go after every ambitious idea that you have, and know that you will sometimes fail, and that is okay—and then sometimes you will succeed beautifully! That's life, but just keep going so that you can live the life you dream

235

of living. *Why not?* You, my friend, have nothing to lose and everything to gain.

You are a shining star emanating like the sun, go out into this world and fulfill your purpose. . .

I BELIEVE IN YOU!

Love from your friend, coach, colleague,
and cheerleader,

Genesis Hey Krick, Founder of Genesis Speaks

Contact and Connect with Genesis directly at info@genesisspeaks.com

Genesis leads small groups to empower women and unleash their potential in all areas of their lives! She hosts speaking engagements, and provides leadership training to women. Invite her to speak to your group, your training, your retreat. To connect with Genesis, please email her at:

You can also email: **genesis@genesisspeaks.com**

Website: **http://genesisspeaks.com**

Phone: **312-772-5453**

Mailing address: 330 Eagle Dr., Rochelle, ILL 61068

Social Media:

Linked In: https://www.linkedin.com/in/genesishey/

Facebook: https://www.facebook.com/genesisspeaks/

YouTube: https://www.youtube.com/user/ShineOnWomen

https://www.youtube.com/user/GDHCareer-Center

Twitter - https://twitter.com/genesishey

BIO

Genesis Hey has her undergraduate degree in marketing and her master's degree in organizational leadership; she is an entrepreneur at heart. As a certified life and career coach, she loves life! She has experienced the sometimes harsh reality of challenges and has discovered how to overcome them—and she knows the true joy of success! She is also certified through "Lay Servant Ministries" and serves as a lay servant leader.

She is a speaker on the national scene, author of two other books, *Hey, Do You Need Exposure?*— which is geared toward helping businesses effectively sell online through video marketing, and

Shine On: A 60 Day Devotional to Discover Your Worth in Christ, a book that inspires and guides young women to recognize their self-worth and claim personal peace amidst mistakes, negative voices from the past, or the stress of many roles and responsibilities. Ultimately, Genesis' mission is to see all women utilize their gifts and live out their individual purpose on this earth. Her desire is to influence positive life change in individuals and businesses by helping them take action through proven success strategies—and for believers, a steady faith in God.

Genesis wants you to remember, *"You can unleash and increase your potential in this life one step at a time!"* Genesis treasures family life with her husband, Jay, and boys Asher and Alistar. In her free time, Genesis loves to read and write, go for morning runs—all the while doing her best to keep up with her growing family.

Made in United States
Troutdale, OR
07/23/2023

11489604R00146